Animal Knits
for Kids

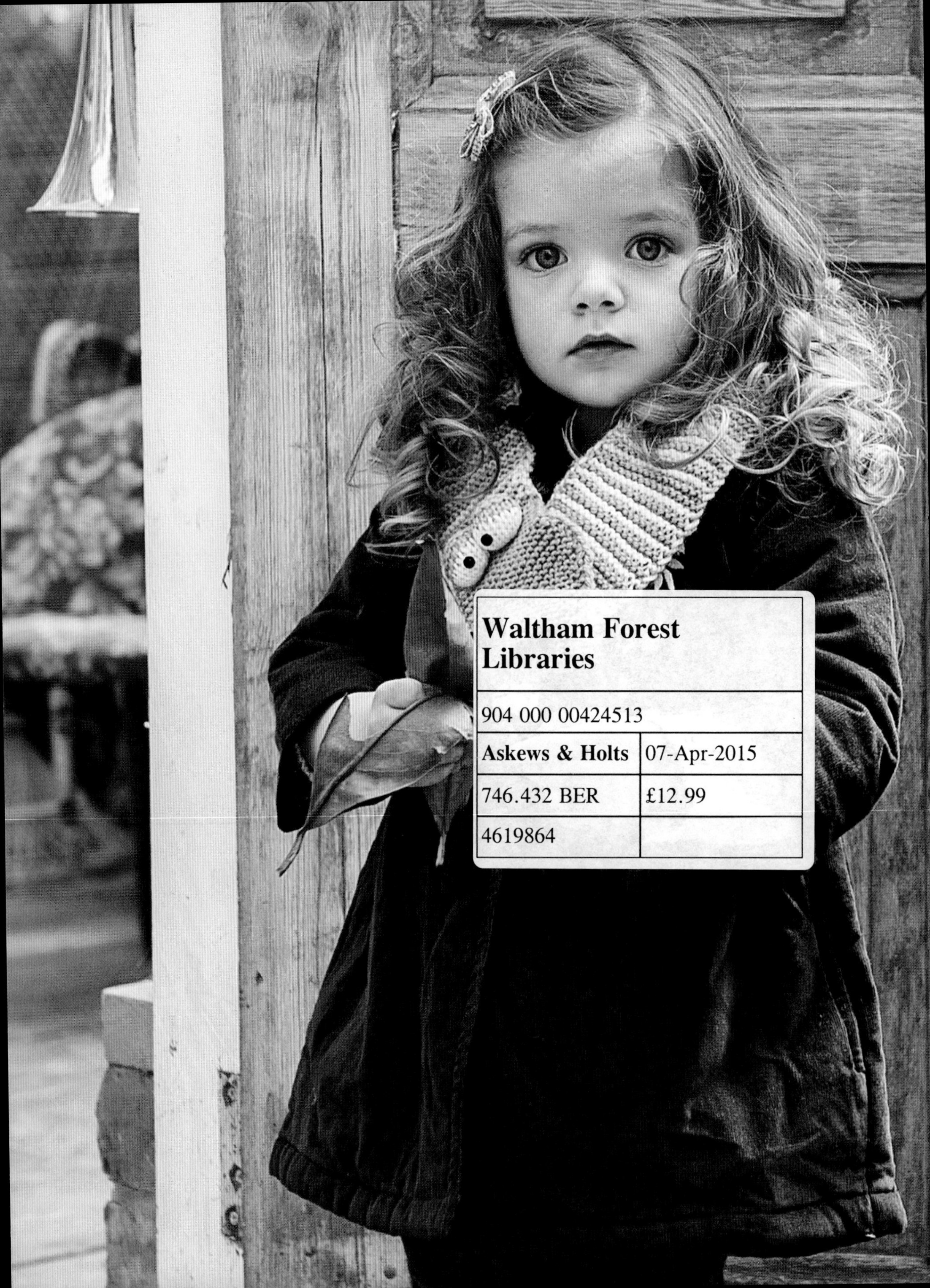

Animal Knits
for Kids

30 Animal Wearables and Toys

Amanda Berry

APPLE

Contents

Chapter 4
Polar Regions

67 Arctic Headbands

71 Polar Bear Paw Print Shoes and Mittens

75 Penguin Baby Bottle Carrier and Toy

79 Penguin Mittens

Chapter 5
Tropical Seas

85 Under-the-Sea Bib

86 Tropical Fish Toys

89 Sea Turtle Coasters

90 Tropical Waves Baby Blanket

93 Shark Bodywarmer

Chapter 6
In the Forest

99 Fox Bib

100 Owl Pillow

105 Reindeer Antler Hat

109 Robin Mittens

113 Owl Sweater, Toy and Scarf

Introduction

This book takes a journey around the animal world, with projects including clothing and accessories for both your baby and your nursery, suitable for girls and boys from newborn to toddler.

Starting with an adventurer outfit to get baby ready for exploring, each chapter travels around the different climate zones of the knitted zoo. On the way, you will encounter animals from the jungle, meet some friendly snakes and crocodiles in the reptile house, experience the tropical seas in the aquarium, feed the penguins in the polar region and end your adventure by meeting some forest animals.

There are several cute knits that could be completed in a day or even an afternoon, as well as bigger projects for the more adventurous knitter. A range of skills and techniques are explored in each project, and each is given a yarn rating with a brief summary of skills involved to give you a heads up before you start. At the back of the book you'll find guidance on the techniques used to help you along the way, as well as several helpful reference charts.

The yarns used can be easily sourced from yarn and craft shops, and vary across a range of weights from fingering weight to chunky. To help you find a suitable yarn for your projects, the yarn band details are also included in the references at the end of the book.

With an eye on your purse, this book also shares some handy hints, such as making use of household items you already own, and how to use waste yarn as a stitch holder, so you don't have to buy lots of new equipment to finish a project.

These projects can be easily adapted to change the size and colours, so you can make some beautiful gifts with your own creative touch. I hope you have as much fun knitting your animals as I did! Amanda

STAR RATING GUIDE

Each project is rated 1 (easy) to 5 (more advanced). Here is a guide to some of the techniques used for each rating:

knit stitches, cast on, cast off

changing colours and knitting stripes, increases and decreases

work in the round, intarsia and Fair Isle colourwork, short rows

cable knitting

multiple techniques

Tool Kit

In addition to yarn, here are the basic tools you will need for these projects.

Knitting needles

Needles can be made from metal, bamboo or plastic. I prefer metal needles as they are more durable.

The size of the needle refers to the diameter of the needle, and for each project the needle size is stated. Straight needles usually have the needle size stamped or printed on them. A needle gauge is a handy tool to help you check the size of your needles, as circular and double pointed needles tend not to be marked with the size.

There are three types of needle: straight, circular and double pointed needles (DPNs). Straight needles are used in pairs to work flat knitting. Double pointed needles are usually sold in sets of four or five and are used to knit circular pieces (called working in the round) and to make I-cords (see page 131). Circular needles are a pair of needles joined by a nylon wire. These can be used to knit in the round, but also to work flat knitting when you have a large number of stitches that may be too big to fit on to straight needles.

Scissors

A pair of small scissors is essential for snipping the yarn and cutting felt pieces. I always keep my scissors in a small case when not in use to prevent any accidents.

Tip You do not need to invest in dressmaker's scissors; a sharp pair of nail scissors will be suitable for most projects.

Sewing needles

To sew knitted pieces together, you will generally use the same yarn that you used to knit the pieces. A tapestry or darning needle with a large eye is used, as the yarn will be too thick to fit through the eye of a regular sewing needle. To sew on buttons, use a regular sewing needle and cotton thread.

Pins

Use pins to hold your knitted pieces together before sewing. I prefer pearl-headed pins as these are easy to spot and tend not to get lost inside your stitches.

Row counter

A row counter is a plastic dial that fits on to the end of a straight needle. You rotate the dial to record the number of rows worked.

Tip You can use a notebook and pencil instead, or even download a row counter app for your smartphone, which is much more fun!

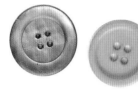

Buttons

Make sure you use a button that will fit through your worked buttonhole. I usually buy my buttons after finishing a project and take my knitting to the craft shop with me to check that the button will fit.

Toy filling

Choose your filling carefully. Polyester filling/stuffing is a popular choice and is a synthetic fibre that is light and usually machine washable. Cotton wool or bamboo filling can also be used, but avoid using pellets or bean bag filling. These have small pieces that are not suitable for babies or young children, as they could be swallowed. For safety, always look for certification marks on your chosen filling.

Tape measure/ruler

A clear plastic ruler is handy for checking tension and measuring small pieces, and a dressmaker's measuring tape is vital for measuring longer and curved pieces.

Stitch holders

Stitch holders are used to hold live stitches, and these usually look like large safety pins.

> 🖋 If you don't have a stitch holder, thread the live stitches on to a spare piece of yarn and knot the ends together. When you need to work the stitches, thread the stitches back on to a knitting needle and pull out the waste yarn.

Stitch markers

These are coloured rings that will mark a position on your row/round of knitting. You can buy them in a multitude of designs.

> 🖋 Instead of buying markers, knot a short length of yarn into a loop and use this as a marker.

Notepad and pencil

I keep a knitting notebook in my work box so I can note any pattern adjustments or other notes as I work. I use a pencil instead of a pen so that I don't mark my knitting by mistake. (I once had a nasty accident with a leaky ballpoint pen that ruined weeks of work … never again!)

Chapter 1

Safari Adventurer

To start our animal adventure, baby will need a safari outfit, complete with desert boots. The satchel will carry all your little explorer's essentials (or a favourite toy).

Combat Trousers

These combat trousers for your little adventurer have a pocket on the leg to hold emergency rations, and can also be teamed up with the jacket project on page 15.

Size: 6–9 months (hips 52 cm/20½ in, length 43 cm/17 in); 12–18 months (hips 54 cm/21¼ in, length 45 cm/17¾ in); 24–36 months (hips 56 cm/22 in, length 47 cm/18½ in). Sample shown is 12–18 months

Yarn: Stylecraft Special Aran (100% acrylic; 100 g/3½ oz; 196 m/214 yd) MC parchment beige (shade 1218) 100 g (3½ oz); CC camel brown (shade 1420) 100 g (3½ oz)

Needles: 4.5 mm (US 7) and 5 mm (US 8) 40 cm (16 in) circular needles, 4.5 mm (US 7) dpns and 5 mm (US 8) straight needles

Notions: Stitch holder

Tension: 10 cm (4 in) square = 18 sts x 24 rows in stocking stitch on 5 mm (US 8) needles with MC

Construction: Worked in the round

Skills needed: Knitting stripes and working short rows

Knitting Pattern

WAISTBAND
Worked in the round from the top down.
With MC and 4.5 mm (US 7) circular needles cast on 106(110,114) sts and join in round. The beg of the rnd is at the centre back of the trousers.
Rnd 1: *K1, P1* to last st.
Rep Rnd 1 for 4 cm (1½ in).
Next rnd: Change to 5 mm (US 8) needles, **K2(3,4), *K2tog, K5* 7 times, K2(3,4) rep from ** to end. (92 (96,100) sts)

SEAT
PM at beg of rnd, K7(7,8), turn (see tip), P14(14,16), turn, K21(21,24) turn, P28(28,32) turn, K35(35,40) turn, P42(42,48) turn, K49(49,56) turn, P56(56,64) turn, K to marker. (92 (96,100) sts)

> **Tip** When wrapping and turning stitches, before each turn, slip the next stitch on the left-hand needle to the right-hand needle, wrap the working yarn around it, then slip the stitch back on to the left needle. Then turn the work. Whenever you reach the stitch with a wrap, pick that wrap up and work it together with the stitch it's wrapping.

TOP OF TROUSERS

Foll rows: work in St st in the round in stripes of CC and MC changing col at the beg of every 2nd round. When the piece measures 18(19,20) cm (7(7½,8) in) from the waist at mid-front, PM after 46(48,50) sts to mark mid-front.

Next rnd: K1, M1, *K to 1 st before marker, M1, K1*, slip marker, K1, M1, rep from * to *. (96(100,104) sts)

Next rnd: K.

Rep the last 2 rnds 3 times (108(112,116) sts) until the mid-front measures 21(22,23) cm (8¼(8½,9) in) long.

LEGS

Starting at mid-back, K the first 54(56,58) sts and slip the rem sts for the other leg on to a stitch holder. *PM on the inside of the leg to mark beg of round. Work in the round in St st on 5 mm (US 8) dpns. When the leg measures 3 cm (1¼ in) work a dec rnd as follows: ssk, K to 2 sts before marker, K2tog. Repeat the dec every 8 rnds three times (46(48,50) sts). Work in St st until the whole piece measures 38(40,42) cm (15(15¾,16½) in) at mid-front, or desired length less 6 cm (2½ in). Change to 4.5 mm (US 7) dpns and work K1, P1 rib in the round for 6 cm (2½ in), then bind off loosely. Rep from * to make the second leg.

POCKET

With MC and 5 mm (US 8) straight needles, cast on 12(14,16) sts and work St st in rows until the piece is square. Cast off. Sew the pocket to one side of the trousers with the cast off edge at the top.

 To knit jogless stripes in the round, on the first colour change round, change colours by simply starting to knit with the new colour after the marker. On the next round, when you come to the marker, slip it. Then, slip the first stitch of the new colour from the left needle to the right needle purlwise. Knit the rest of the stitches of the round. Repeat as required.

Adventurer Jacket

A unisex jacket with the front and back knitted in one piece to minimise seaming. It features a garter stitch trim and placket.

Knitting Pattern

FRONT AND BACK

With MC and 5 mm (US 8) circular needles, cast on 88(92,96) sts. Work flat (do not join in the round).

Rows 1 to 5: K.

Foll rows: starting and ending with a P [WS] row, work St st until piece measures 20(21,22) cm (8(8¼,8½) in) from the cast on edge.

Next RS row: K16(17,18) (right front), cast off 4 sts (armhole), K48(50,52) (back), cast off 4 sts (armhole), K16(17,18) (left front). (80(84,88) sts)

LEFT FRONT

Starting with a P [WS] row, work in St st on the 16(17,18) sts for 11(11,12) cm (4½(4½,4¾) in), transfer the sts to a stitch holder.

Size: 6–9 months (chest 54 cm/21¼ in, length 31 cm/12¼ in); 12–18 months (chest 56 cm/22 in, length 32 cm/12½ in); 24–36 months (chest 58 cm/22¾ in, length 34 cm/13½ in). Sample shown is 12–18 months

Yarn: Stylecraft Special Aran (100% acrylic; 100 g/3½ oz; 196 m/214 yd) MC camel brown (shade 1420) 200 g (7 oz)

Other materials: 7 domed buttons (14 mm/½ in diameter)

Needles: 5 mm (US 8) 40 cm (16 in) circular needles, 5 mm (US 8) dpns and 5 mm (US 8) straight needles

Notions: stitch holder

Tension: 10 cm (4 in) square = 18 sts x 24 rows in stocking stitch on 5 mm (US 8) needles with MC

Construction: Worked flat (back and forth) using a circular needle to accommodate the no. of sts, and worked in the round

Skills needed: Picking up stitches, working in the round

BACK

Starting with a P [WS] row, work in St st on the 48(50,52) sts for 11(11,12) cm (4½(4½,4¾) in), transfer the sts to a stitch holder.

RIGHT FRONT

Work as for left front.

SHOULDERS

Join the shoulder seams by grafting the 16(17,18) sts for the fronts to 16(17,18) sts at the ends of the back piece, and hold the middle 16 sts at the back for the collar.

PLACKETS – MAKE 1 ON EACH FRONT EDGE

With RS of the front side edge facing you, pick up 3 sts every 4 rows between the cast on edge to 4(4.5,6.5) cm (1½(1¾,2½) in) below the top shoulder seam. Work these sts in garter stitch until the placket measures 5.5(6.5,7.5) cm (2(2½,3) in) wide. Make the buttonholes at 6.5 cm (2½ in) and 9.5 cm (3¾ in) from the top edge by working a YO followed by K2tog. Buttonholes need to be on the left front for boys and the right front for girls. Continue working these sts until placket measures 7(8,9) cm (2¾(3,3½) in) wide. Cast off all placket sts.

Placket buttonholes: Make two eyelet buttonholes when the placket is 5.5(6.5,7.5) cm (2(2½,3) in) wide.

COLLAR

With the RS facing you, pick up 3 sts every 4 rows on the side edge above the placket to the shoulder seam, k the 16 held sts at the back, then pick up the sts on the other side edge up to the placket. Work these collar sts in garter stitch until the collar measures 5(6,7) cm (2(2½,2¾) in) wide. Cast off all collar sts.

SLEEVES – MAKE 2

Starting at the centre of the underarm, pick up 3 sts every 4 rows around the armhole and 4 sts at the bottom of the armhole. Transfer to 5 mm (US 8) dpns and, working in the round, K every rnd, and dec by 2 sts every 10th rnd four times as follows: K1, ssk, K to 3 sts before end of rnd, K2tog, K1. Work until sleeve measures 16(17.5,19) cm (6¼(6¾,7½) in) from underarm then work 5 rnds in garter stitch (P and K alt rnds). Cast off all sleeve sts.

TABS – MAKE 3

With MC and 5 mm (US 8) straight needles, cast on 11 sts.
Row 1 and every alt row: K.
Rows 2,4, and 6: K1, kfb, K rem sts. (14 sts)
Rows 8,10, and 12: K1, K2tog, K rem sts. (11 sts)
Cast off all sts.

FINISHING

Weave in any yarn tails. Sew the tabs on the front side pieces and one at the centre back of the jacket. Sew buttons under buttonholes on the placket and 2(1.25,1.25) cm (¾(½,½) in) from the other edge of the placket and one button on top of each tab.

Desert Boots

Lace up desert boots for your young adventurer.
To make these boots for newborns, follow the pattern using smaller needles and a DK or Aran weight yarn.

Size: 3–12 months (length 10.5 cm/4¼ in, width 7 cm/2¾ in, height 7 cm/2¾ in)

Yarn: Stylecraft Special Chunky (100% acrylic; 100 g/3¼ oz; 144 m/157 yd) MC meadow green (shade 1065) 25 g (1 oz); CC1 camel brown (shade 1420) 25 g (1 oz); Sirdar Hayfield Bonus DK (100% acrylic; 100 g/3½ oz; 280 m/306 yd) CC2 fox orange (shade 779) 10 g (½ oz)

Needles: 5 mm (US 8) dpns and 5 mm (US 8) straight needles; 2 x 3.25mm (US 3) dpns

Notions: Stitch holder

Tension: 10 cm (4 in) square = 16 sts x 22 rows in stocking stitch on 5 mm (US 8) needles with MC

Construction: Worked flat and in the round

Skills needed: Making an I-cord, yarnover increases, decreases

Knitting Pattern

BOOTS – MAKE 2

SOLE

With CC1 and 5 mm (US 8) dpns cast on 22 sts and join in the round.

Rnds 1, 3, 5, 7, and 9: P.

Rnd 2: K3, *M1, K1* 3 times, K8, M1, K2, M1, K6. (27 sts)

Rnd 4: K3, M1, K2, *M1, K3* 2 times, K6, M1, K4, M1, K6. (32 sts)

Rnd 6: K3, *M1, K4* 3 times, K5, M1, K6, M1, K6. (37 sts)

Rnd 8: K3, M1, K5, *M1, K6* 2 times, K3, M1, K8, M1, K6. (42 sts)

Rnds 10 to 14: Join MC, K.

Rnd 15: K3, *ssk, K2* 2 times, *K2tog, K2* 2 times, sl1 pwise, byf, turn. (38 sts)

Rnd 16: Sl1 pwise, byf, P14, sl1 pwise, tyb, turn.

Rnd 17: Sl1 pwise, tyb, K2, ssk, K1, ssk, *K2tog, K1* 2 times, sl1 pwise, byf, turn. (34 sts)

Rnd 18: Sl1 pwise, byf, P8, sl1 pwise, tyb, turn.

Rnd 19: Sl1 pwise, tyb, *ssk* 2 times, *K2tog* 2 times, pick up wrap and K together with next st twice, K to end of rnd. (30 sts)

Rnd 20: Pick up wrap and K together with next st twice, K to end of rnd, turn.

Arrange stitches: place the first 22 sts on a 5 mm (US 8) straight needle for the back of shoe, and transfer the last 8 sts for the tongue to a stitch holder.

BACK OF SHOE

Work the 22 sts back and forth (flat) in MC and start with the WS facing you.

Row 21: K1, M1, yo, P2tog, P16, yo, P2tog, M1, K1. (24 sts)

Row 22 and every alt row: K.

Row 23: K2, P to last 2 sts, K2.

Row 25: K2, yo, P2tog, P16, yo, P2tog, K2. (24 sts)

Row 27: Rep row 23.

Row 29: Rep row 25.

Row 31: Rep row 22.

Cast off the 24 sts

TONGUE

Work the 8 held sts back and forth (flat) in MC and start with the RS facing you.

Row 21: Kfbf, K6, Kfbf. (12 sts)

Rows 22 to 30: Starting and ending with a P row, work St st for 9 rows.

Row 31: K4, ssk, K2tog, K4. (10 sts)

Rows 32 and 34: P.

Row 33: K3, ssk, K2tog, K3. (8 sts)

Cast off 8 sts.

LACES – MAKE 2

With 2 (size 3.25mm/US 3) dpns and CC2, cast on 3 sts and make I-cord 34 cm (13½ in) long (see page 131). Cast off.

FINISHING

Sew the seam at the bottom of the sole and thread the I-cord laces through the eyelets.

 Kfbf is a double increase: knit into the front and then the back of the next stitch, and then into the front again, to make an additional 2 sts.

Safari Satchel

This garter stitch satchel will hold your adventurer's favourite toys while also keeping your play area tidy!

Knitting Pattern

STRAP – MAKE 1
With CC1 and 5 mm (US 8) needles, cast on 8 sts and work garter stitch for 68 cm (26¾ in) or required strap length. Cast off.

BODY – MAKE 1
With MC and 5 mm (US 8) needles, cast on 26 sts and work garter stitch for 29 cm (11½ in). Cast off.

SIDES – MAKE 2
With MC and 5 mm (US 8) needles, cast on 8 sts and work garter stitch for 8.5 cm (3¼ in). Cast off.

TABS – MAKE 2
With CC2 and 5 mm (US 8) needles, cast on 6 sts and work garter stitch for 3 cm (1¼ in).
Next row: K3, yo, K2tog, K1. (6 sts)
Next 2 rows: K.
Cast off.

FINISHING
Line up the cast on edges of the body and side pieces and sew the side edge of each side piece to the body. Wrap the body piece around the bottom and other side edge of each side piece and sew together. The remainder of the bag body piece is the front flap. Sew the tabs on to the front flap, and sew the ends of the strap to the back of the bag. Sew buttons on to the bag front under the buttonhole tabs.

> *Tip*
> To work garter stitch, knit every row. For a neater finish to the edges of garter stitch pieces, slip the last stitch of every row purlwise with the yarn in the front of the work.

Size: 14 cm (5½ in) wide, 9 cm (3½ in) high and 4 cm (1½ in) deep

Yarn: Stylecraft Special Aran (100% acrylic; 100 g/3½ oz; 196 m/214 yd) MC meadow green (shade 1065) 50 g (2 oz); CC1 camel brown (shade 1420) 50 g (2 oz); CC2 parchment beige (shade 1218) 50 g (2 oz)

Other materials: 2 buttons (12 mm/½ in diameter)

Needles: 5 mm (US 8) straight needles

Notions: Darning or tapestry needle

Tension: 10 cm (4 in) square = 18 sts x 36 rows on 5 mm (US 8) needles in garter stitch with MC

Construction: Worked flat

Skills needed: Seaming, eyelet buttonholes

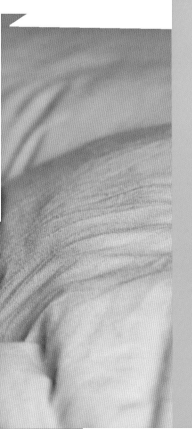

Chapter 2

In the jungle

Here we will meet some friendly monkeys, hippos, rhinos, elephants and tigers. Projects include footwear, headgear and this adorable – yet challenging – onesie.

Monkey and Hippo Rattles

These little knitted rattles with striped handles are made from the same basic pattern. Intarsia colourwork is used to make the monkey's eyes.

Knitting Pattern

MONKEY

RATTLE – MAKE 1
With CC1 and 4 mm (US 6) needles cast on 7 sts.
Rows 1 and 3: P.
Row 2: K1, *kfb* 6 times. (13 sts)
Row 4: K1, *kfb, K1* 6 times. (19 sts)
Rows 5 to 26: Join MC and work stripes of 2 rows MC then 2 rows CC1, and rep sequence. Starting with a P row, work in St st for 22 rows.
Row 27: With CC1, *P2tog* 9 times, P1. (10 sts)
Row 28: Join CC2. K1, *kfb* 9 times. (19 sts)
Row 29 and every foll alt row: P with CC2.
Row 30: With CC2, K1, *kfb* 18 times. (37 sts)
Row 32: With CC2, K5, kfb, *K8, kfb* 3 times, K4. (41 sts)
Row 34: With CC2, K5, kfb, *K9, kfb* 3 times, K5. (45 sts)
Rows 35 to 41: With CC2 and starting and ending with a P row, work in St st for 7 rows.
Row 42: With CC2 K5, *ssk, K9, K2tog*, K9, rep from * to *, K5. (41 sts)
Row 44: With CC2 K5, *ssk* 2 times, K1, K2tog, K1, *K2tog* 2 times, K7, *ssk* 2 times, K1, ssk, K1, *K2tog* 2 times, K5. (31 sts)
Row 45: Work eyes in intarsia. MC P12, CC2 P7, MC P12.
Row 46: MC K12, CC2 K7, MC K12.
Row 47: Rep Row 45.
Row 48: MC K13, CC2 K5, MC K13.
Work all rem rows in MC.
Rows 49 to 53: Starting and ending with a P row, work in St st for 5 rows.
Row 54: K1, *K2tog, K1* 10 times. (21 sts)
Row 56: *K2tog* 10 times, K1. (11 sts)
Break yarn, thread through sts and gather to cast off. Sew side edges together, adding stuffing as you sew, and finish by gathering the cast on sts at the bottom of the rattle handle. Embroider the mouth with black yarn and sew black buttons on top of small white felt circles for eyes and attach to the rattle.

Size: approx. 15 x 7 cm (6 x 2¾ in)

Yarn: Sirdar Hayfield Bonus DK (100% acrylic; 100 g/3½ oz; 280 m/306 yd).
Monkey: MC wheat brown (shade 816) 25 g (1 oz); CC1 white (shade 961) 25 g (1 oz); CC2 bright lemon yellow (shade 819) 25 g (1 oz)
Hippo: MC powder blue (shade 960) 25 g (1 oz); CC1 white (shade 961) 25 g (1 oz)

Other materials: 50 g (2 oz) polyester toy filling for each rattle, 2 buttons (6 mm/¼ in diameter) for eyes for each rattle, small disks of white felt, and black wool for embroidery

Needles: 4 mm (US 6) straight needles

Notions: Darning or tapestry needle

Tension: 10 cm (4 in) square = 22 sts x 28 rows in stocking stitch on 4 mm (US 6) needles with MC

Construction: Worked flat

Skills needed: Knitting stripes, seaming; intarsia colourwork for the monkey's face

MONKEY EARS – MAKE 2
With MC and 4 mm (US 6) needles cast on 15 sts.
Rows 1, 3, and 5: P.
Row 2: *K2tog, K1* to end. (10 sts)
Row 4: *K2tog* to end. (5 sts)
Break yarn, thread through sts, gather to cast off at the inside of the ear and sew the side edges together to make a circle. Sew an ear to each side of the monkey's head.

HIPPO
Work as for Monkey, working Rows 28 to 56 in MC only. Embroider small circles for the nostrils on the front of the face. For the ears, work as for the monkey ears but cast on 12 sts in MC, decrease to 4 sts and sew to the top of the head.

Tiger Onesie

This hooded onesie in tiger stripes with matching tiger-stripe socks (see page 30) will keep baby warm. Knitted in garter stitch, this pattern incorporates intarsia colourwork and stripes, but you could make it in one colour for an easier knit. Although this is worked flat, where there are a lot of stitches to work for the body, you may find it easier to work back and forth on a circular needle.

Size: 0–3 months (chest 46 cm/18 in); 3–6 months (chest 50 cm/19¾ in); 6–12 months (chest 54 cm/21¼ in). Sample shown is 0–3 months

Yarn: Sirdar Hayfield Bonus DK (100% acrylic; 100 g/3½ oz; 280 m/306 yd) MC bright orange (shade 981) 100 g (3½ oz); CC1 white (shade 961) 100 g (3½ oz); CC2 dark grey mix (shade 790) 100 g (3½ oz). Darker orange sample (page 29) uses MC fox (shade 779)

Other materials: 5 buttons (15 mm/½ in diameter) for front fastening

Needles: 4.5 mm (US 7) and 5 mm (US 8) straight needles, and 5 mm (US 8) 40 cm (16 in) circular needles

Notions: Stitch holders (or you could use spare circular needles or waste pieces of yarn)

Tension: 10 cm (4 in) square = 20 sts x 40 rows in garter stitch on 5 mm (US 8) needles with MC

Construction: Worked flat and in the round

Skills needed: Buttonholes, intarsia colourwork, knitting stripes and picking up stitches

Knitting Pattern

LEFT LEG – MAKE 1

With 4.5 mm (US 7) needles and CC1, cast on 34(38,42) sts.

Rows 1 to 8: *K1, P1* to end.

Change to 5 mm (US 8) needles.

Row 9: [WS] K.

Change to MC.

Rows 10 to 17: K.

Joining new colours as required, work in stripes in the foll sequence: 2 rows CC1, 6 rows CC2, 2 rows CC1, 8 rows MC, and rep sequence.

Row 18: Kfb, K to last st, kfb. (36(40,44) sts)

Rows 19 to 21: K.

Rep Rows 18–21 until you have 52(56,60) sts, then cont working in garter stitch until the leg measures 19(22,26) cm (7½(8½,10¼) in), ending with WS row.

Next RS row: cast off the first 4 sts, K to last 4 sts, cast off the last 4 sts. (44(48,52) sts.

Work 6 rows in garter stitch ** then place the 44(48,52) sts on a stitch holder. They will be used for the front.

RIGHT LEG – MAKE 1

Work as for left leg to **. Place right and left leg sts on a 5 mm (US 8) circular needle with WS facing you. Work on these (88(96,104)) sts for the body, working the first buttonhole after working 3 cm (1¼ in) of the body, and subsequent buttonholes every 6 cm (2½ in) after that.

For boys, work buttonholes on RS rows by casting off the 3rd and 4th sts from the end of the row. On the next [WS] row K2, then cast on 2 new sts over the cast off sts.

For girls, cast off the 3rd and 4th sts from the beg of the RS row, and cast on 2 sts over these sts on the next WS row.

BODY – MAKE 1

Work flat (back and forth) and cont stripes col sequence but K the first and last 6 sts on all rows in CC1 for the button band using the intarsia method (see page 133) to change colours.

Row 1: Cast on 4 sts in CC1 at the beg of the row, in CC1 K6, in stripe col K to last 2 sts, in CC1 K2, and cast on 4 sts at the end of the row. (96(104,112) sts)

Work in garter stitch in stripes until the piece measures 42(45,49) cm (16½(17¾,19¼) in), ending with a WS row. These sts are allocated as 26(28,30) sts for left front, 44(48,52) sts for the back and 26(28,30) sts for the right front.

LEFT FRONT

Cont in stripes col sequence but work the first 6 sts in CC1 for the button band on RS rows and the last 6 sts in CC1 on WS rows.

Row 1: [RS] K26(28,30), place the rem sts on a holder. They will be used for back and right front.

Rows 2 to 12: Work in garter stitch, and on all WS rows cast on sts for sleeve as follows:

Row 2: Cast on 2 sts, K to end.

Rows 4 and 6: Cast on 3 sts, K to end.

Rows 8 and 10: Cast on 4 sts, K to end.

Row 12: Cast on 12 sts. (54(56,58) sts)

Rows 13 to 17: K.

Row 18: [WS] K to last 6 sts, place last 6 sts of button band on a stitch holder (they will be used for the hood). (48(50,52) sts)

Continue to work in the stripes col sequence while working left front neckline.

Row 1: Ssk, K to end. (47(49,51) sts)

Row 2: K.

Rep these 2 rows until 42(44,46) sts remain. Then work in garter stitch until the armhole is 9(10,11.5) cm (3½(4,4½) in) deep. Cast off.

BACK

Start with the RS facing you and work in the stripes col sequence.

Row 1: [RS] Transfer the 44(48,52) sts for the back from the stitch holder to the needles. Leave the rem sts for the right front on the stitch holder. K44(48,52) sts.

Row 2: Cast on 2 sts at the beg of row, K rem sts, cast on 2 sts at the end of row. (48(52,56) sts)

Row 3: K to last st, cast on 3 sts.

Row 4: K to last st, cast on 3 sts.

Row 5: K to last st, cast on 3 sts.

Row 6: K to last st, cast on 3 sts.

Row 7: K to last st, cast on 4 sts.

Row 8: K to last st, cast on 4 sts.

Row 9: K to last st, cast on 4 sts.

Row 10: K to last st, cast on 4 sts.

Row 11: K to last st, cast on 12 sts.

Row 12: K to last st, cast on 12 sts. (100(104,108) sts)

Continue to work in garter stitch until the armhole depth is 9(10,11.5) cm (3½(4,4½) in) and the back is the same length as the left front. Cast off.

RIGHT FRONT

Cont in the stripes col sequence but work the first 6 sts in CC1 for the button band on WS rows and the last 6 sts in CC1 on RS rows. Transfer the 26(28,30) sts for the right front from the stitch holder to the needles.

Row 1: [RS] K26(28,30).

Rows 2 to 17: repeat as for left front, casting on sts at the end (not the beg) of the row on all WS rows. (54(56,58) sts)

Row 18: K.

Row 19: [RS] K to last 8 sts, K2tog, place the last 6 sts of the button band on a stitch holder until you are ready to work hood. (47(49,51) sts)

Work rem rows of right front in stripes col sequence for the neckline.

Row 1: [WS] K.

Row 2: K to last 2 sts, K2tog. (46(48,50) sts)

Rep these 2 rows until 42 (44,46) sts remain, then work in garter stitch until the armhole depth is 9(10,11.5) cm (3½(4,4½) in). Cast off. Sew together the top seam of the sleeves to join the front and back.

CUFFS

With RS facing, using CC1 and 4.5 mm (US 7) straight needles, pick up an odd number of sts evenly across the end of one sleeve.

Row 1: *K1, P1* to last st, K1.

Row 2: *P1, K1* to last st, P1.

Rep Rows 1 and 2 until the cuff measures 3.5 cm (1¼ in), then cast off loosely. Rep for other sleeve, then sew the bottom sleeve seams to join the inner arm.

HOOD – MAKE 1

Place the 6 sts from the left front button band on a 5 mm (US 8) needle with the WS facing you.

Row 1: K6 in CC1, then pick up an even number of sts around the neckline and the back of the body using MC, then place the 6 held sts from the right front button band on the needle.

Work the first and last 6 sts of every row in CC1 and the rem sts in MC. Work in garter stitch until the hood measures 20(23,26) cm (8(9,10¼) in).

Divide the stitches evenly between two needles and graft the top of the hood together.

EARS – MAKE 2

With 5 mm (US 8) needles and CC2, cast on 30 sts. Work rows 1 and 2 with CC2 and rem rows with CC1.

Row 1 and every alt. row: K.

Row 2: *K2tog, K3* to end of row. (24 sts)

Row 4: *K2tog, K2* to end of row. (18 sts)

Row 6: *K2tog, K1* to end of row. (12 sts)

Row 8: *K2tog* to end of row. (6 sts)

Break yarn, thread through sts and gather to cast off. Stitch the side edges of the ears to the top of the hood, so that the cast on edge forms the outer edge of the ear.

FINISHING

Sew the inner leg seam and sew across crotch, then sew buttons under the buttonholes at the front.

Tiger-stripe Socks

These tiger socks are knitted from the toe up in blocks of stripes. You can make the socks smaller by using smaller 3.5 mm (US 4) needles and a lighter weight yarn, or make them bigger by using larger 4.5 mm (US 7) needles and a heavier weight yarn. If you are new to knitting socks, you may find it easier to work the pattern in one colour or self-striping yarn.

Size: 3–6 months
(length 10–11 cm/4–4½ in)

Yarn: Sirdar Hayfield Bonus DK (100% acrylic; 100 g/3½ oz; 280 m/306 yd) MC white (shade 961) 25 g (1 oz); CC1 dark grey mix (shade 790) 25 g (1 oz); CC2 bright orange (shade 981) 25 g (1 oz)

Needles: 4 mm (US 6) dpns

Tension: 10 cm (4 in) square = 22 sts x 28 rows in stocking stitch on 4 mm (US 6) needles with MC

Construction: Worked in the round

Skills needed: Short rows, wrapping and turning stitches

Knitting Pattern

SOCKS – MAKE 2

With CC1 and 4 mm (US 6) dpns cast on 12 sts divided between 2 dpns as follows: hold the dpns parallel and cast 6 sts on to each of the two needles, cast the 1st stitch on to the front needle, the 2nd on to the back needle, and repeat to join the toe seam.

Rnd 1: K and arrange the sts on 3 dpns: 6 sts (instep), 3 sts (sole) and 3 sts (sole).

Rnd 2: *K1, M1, K4, M1, K1* twice. (16 sts)

Rnds 3 and 5: K.

Rnd 4: *K1, M1, K6, M1, K1* twice. (20 sts)

Rnd 6: *K1, M1, K8, M1, K1* twice. (24 sts)

Rnd 7: K.

Rnds 8 to 15: K with CC2.

Rnds 16 to 23: K with MC.

Rnd 24: K with CC1.

HEEL

Shape the heel with short row shaping and CC1.

Row 1: K23, w&t last st.

Row 2: P10, w&t.

Row 3: K9, w&t.

Row 4: P8, w&t.

Row 5: K7, w&t.

Row 6: P6, w&t.

Row 7: K6, w&t (wrapped stitch will have 2 loops).

Pick up wraps and work together with st for the foll rows:

Row 8: P7, w&t.

Row 9: K8, w&t.

Row 10: P9, w&t.

Row 11: K11.

Foll rnd: K one rnd in CC1. (24 sts)

LEG

Work the leg in the round:

Rnd 1: K with MC.

Rnd 2: *K2, p2* to end of rnd.

Rep Rnd 2 until the ribbed piece measures 6 cm (2½ in). Cast off loosely.

FINISHING

Weave in the yarn tails.

Tip To wrap and turn (w&t) stitches, work to the point at which you need to turn your work. Slip the next stitch on the left-hand needle to the right-hand needle, wrap the working yarn around it, then slip the stitch back on to the left-hand needle. Turn the work. When you are ready to work the wrapped stitch, pick up the wrap and work it together with the stitch it's wrapping. See pages 128–130 for further help with this.

Elephant Hat

This little hat has a chin strap to keep it on baby's head and an elephant trunk and ears for fun. Knit every row to create garter stitch. Add antlers or bear ears instead to make a collection of animal hats.

Size: 12–36 months (to fit head circumference 44–50 cm/17¼–19½ in)

Yarn: King Cole Big Value Chunky (100% acrylic; 100 g/3½ oz; 152 m/166 yd) MC grey (shade 547) 100 g (3½ oz)

Other materials: 1 button for strap (12 mm/½ in diameter), 2 buttons for eyes (12 mm/½ in diameter) and circles of white felt

Needles: 5 mm (US 8) straight needles

Tension: 10 cm (4 in) square = 15 sts x 24 rows in stocking stitch on 5 mm (US 8) needles with MC

Construction: Worked flat

Skills needed: Increases and decreases, rib patterns, seaming

Knitting Pattern

HAT – MAKE 1

With 5 mm (US 8) needles and MC, cast on 8 sts.

Row 1 and every alt row: P [WS].
Row 2: K1, *kfb* 7 times. (15 sts)
Row 4: K1, *kfb, K1* 7 times. (22 sts)
Row 6: K1, *kfb, K2* 7 times. (29 sts)
Row 8: K1, *kfb, K3* 7 times. (36 sts)
Row 10: K1, *kfb, K4* 7 times. (43 sts)
Row 12: K1, *kfb, K5* 7 times. (50 sts)
Row 14: K1, *kfb, K6* 7 times. (57 sts)
Row 16: K1, *kfb, K7* 7 times. (64 sts)
Row 18: K1, *kfb, K8* 7 times. (71 sts)
Next rows: Work in St st until piece measures 15.5 cm (6 in) long.
Next rows: Work 3 rows in garter st (K every row).
Next row: K23, cast off 25 sts for brim, K rem sts. (46 sts). Break yarn, leaving a 15.5 cm (6 in) yarn tail.

Transfer the two sets of 23 sts on to 1 needle so they join at centre back. With WS facing you, K all sts. (46 sts) Work in garter stitch for 3 cm (1¼ in).
Next row: K6, cast off to the last 6 sts, K6 (12 sts).

On the 6 sts just worked, work garter stitch for 3 cm (1¼ in) to create a strap. Cast off these 6 sts.

With WS facing you, rejoin yarn to remaining 6 sts and work in garter stitch for 18 cm (7 in) or length required for the strap to go under the chin.
Next row (make buttonhole): K2, yo, K2tog, K2. (6 sts)
Work 2 more rows in garter stitch. Cast off.

FINISHING

Sew up the centre back seam of the hat and gather the cast on sts at the top using the yarn tail. Sew a button on to the short tab of the chin strap.

TRUNK – MAKE 1

With 5 mm (US 8) needles and MC, cast on 10 sts.
Row 1: P.
Row 2: *Kfb* 10 times. (20 sts)
Rows 3, 4, and 5: P.
Rows 6 and 7: K.
Rows 8 and 9: P.
Rows 10 to 29: Rep Rows 6–9 five times.

Rows 30 to 31: Rep Rows 6 and 7.
Cast off leaving a 15.5 cm (6 in) yarn tail.
Sew the side edges together and gather the cast on sts at the tip of the trunk using the yarn tail. Sew the cast off edge to the front of the hat and sew on the button and felt eyes above it.

EARS – MAKE 2

With 5 mm (US 8) needles and MC, cast on 9 sts.
Row 1 and every alt row: K.
Row 2: K1, *kfb, K1* to end. (13 sts)
Row 4: K1, *kfb, K2* to end. (17 sts)
Row 6: K1, *kfb, K3* to end. (21 sts)
Row 8: K1, *kfb, K4* to end. (25 sts)
Row 10: K1, *kfb, K5* to end. (29 sts)
Row 12: K1, *K2tog, K5* to end. (25 sts)
Row 14: K1, *K2tog, K4* to end. (21 sts)
Row 16: K1, *K2tog, K3* to end. (17 sts)
Row 18: K1, *K2tog, K2* to end. (13 sts)
Row 20: K1, *K2tog, K1* to end. (9 sts)
Cast off. Sew the cast off edges to the sides of the hat.

Rhino Boots

These little boots have a ribbed cuff to keep them on baby's feet during their busy day at the zoo, and a horn detail to help them stand out in the crowd.

Size: 3–6 months (length 11 cm/4½ in, width 7 cm/2¾ in); 6–12 months (length 13 cm/5 in, width 8 cm/3 in). Sample shown is 3–6 months

Yarn: Stylecraft Special Aran (100% acrylic; 100 g/3½ oz; 196 m/214 yd) MC aster blue (shade 1003) 50 g (2 oz). Sirdar Hayfield Bonus DK (100% acrylic; 100 g/3½ oz; 280 m/306 yd) CC white (shade 961) 20 g (¾ oz)

Other materials: Small amount of toy filling for the horn

Needles: 4 mm (US 6), 4.5 mm (US 7) and 5 mm (US 8) straight knitting needles

Tension: 10 cm (4 in) square = 18 sts x 24 rows in stocking stitch on 5 mm (US 8) needles with MC

Construction: Worked flat

Skills needed: Turning work, seaming and rib patterns

Knitting Pattern

BOOTS – MAKE 2

With 5 mm (US 8) needles and MC, cast on 25(29) sts.
Rows 1, 3, and 5: K.
Row 2: K1, M1, K11(13), M1, K1, M1, K11(13), M1, K1. (29(33) sts)
Row 4: K2, M1, K11(13), M1, K3, M1, K11(13), M1, K2. (33(37) sts)
Row 6: K3, M1, K11(13), M1, K5, M1, K11(13), M1, K3. (37(41) sts)
Foll rows: Work 10(12) rows in garter stitch.

To shape the top of the boot:
Row 1: K22(24), K2tog, sl1, byf, turn. (36(39) sts)
Row 2: Sl1, K8, K2tog, sl1, byf, turn. (35(39) sts)
Rep Row 2 until 25(29) sts rem.
Next row: Sl1, K to last st, M1, K1. (26(30) sts)
Next row: K. Switch to 4.5 mm (US 7) needles.
Next row: *K2, P2* to last 2 sts, K2.
Next row: *P2, K2* to last 2 sts, p2.
Rep the last 2 rows until the ribbed piece is 8(10) cm (3(4) in) long.
Cast off in rib pattern.
Sew the side edges together to join the back seam, then sew the sole seam.

HORN – MAKE 1 FOR EACH BOOT

With 4 mm (US 6) needles and CC cast on 15 sts.
Row 1 and every alt row: [WS] P.
Row 2: K5, K2tog, K1, ssk, K5. (13 sts)
Row 4: K4, K2tog, K1, ssk, K4. (11 sts)
Row 6: K3, K2tog, K1, ssk, K3. (9 sts)
Row 8: K2, K2tog, K1, ssk, K2. (7 sts)
Row 10: K1, K2tog, K1, ssk, K1. (5 sts)
Row 12: K2tog, K1, ssk. (3 sts)
Break yarn leaving a 15.5 cm (6 in) tail. Thread the tail through the sts and gather to cast off. Sew the side edges of the horn together, adding stuffing as you sew. Sew the cast on edge of the horns to the tops of the boots.

Tip The instruction 'byf' means you must bring the working yarn to the front of the work between the needles then work as normal.

Chapter 3

The Reptile House

These reptile knits are cuddly and cute, with baby accessories, toys, winter warmers and some fun little storage baskets to brighten up the nursery.

Snake Scarf

This garter stitch scarf is an easy to pick up and put down project. The stripes are also a great way to use up any odds and ends of yarn you have left over from other projects.

Knitting Pattern

SCARF

HEAD
With 4 mm (US 6) needles and MC cast on 4 sts.
Row 1: K.
Row 2: Kfb, K to last st, kfb. (6 sts)
Rep Rows 1 and 2 until you have 22 sts, then work 9 rows in garter stitch.
Next row: Ssk, K to last 2 sts, K2tog. (20 sts)
Next row: K.
Rep the last 2 rows (18 sts), then work 8 rows in garter stitch **.

BODY
Continue to work on the 18 sts in garter stitch stripes of 2 rows in MC and 2 rows in CC, changing the CC every 5 cm (2 in), until the piece measures 62 cm (24½ in).
You can work any stripe pattern you wish or work in blocks of colour. If you choose to work stripes every 2 rows, carry the unused colour up the side of the work to save having to weave in lots of yarn tails at the end.

Size: 8 cm (3 in) wide, 73 cm (28¾ in) long

Yarn: Sirdar Hayfield Bonus DK (100% acrylic; 100 g/3½ oz; 280 m/306 yd) MC grass green (shade 825) 50 g (2 oz); CC1 white (shade 961) 25 g (1 oz); CC2 classic red (shade 833) 25 g (1 oz); CC (stripe colours): I used a combination of 25 g (1 oz) of the following: bright lemon yellow (shade 819), powder blue (shade 960), fox orange (shade 779), aran cream (shade 993), denim blue (shade 994), iced pink (shade 958), light grey mix (shade 814), lilac (shade 959)

Other materials: 2 buttons (6 mm/¼ in diameter) and a small amount of toy filling

Needles: 4 mm (US 6) straight needles

Tension: 10 cm (4 in) square = 22 sts x 38 rows in garter stitch on 4 mm (US 6) needles with MC

Construction: Worked flat

Skills needed: Increases and decreases, knitting stripes

TAIL

Cont to work on the 18 sts, and work 10 rows in garter stitch in MC.

Next row: Ssk, K to last 2 sts, K2 tog. (18 sts)

Next row: K.

Rep the last 2 rows until 2 sts remain. Cast off.

EYES – MAKE 2

With 4 mm (US 6) needles and MC cast on 6 sts.

Row 1: K.

Row 2: Kfb, K to last st, kfb. (8 sts)

Rep Rows 1 and 2 until you have 12 sts.

Next row: K with MC.

Next row: P with CC1.

Next row: With CC1 K2tog, K to last 2 sts, K2tog. (10 sts)

Rep the last 2 rows until you have 6 sts in CC1.

Break yarn and thread through the sts to cast off. Use the yarn tail to sew a running stitch around the outside edge of the eye. Pull the yarn to gather the stitches together, adding a little stuffing to the inside to make a small bobble. Sew a black button on to the eye and sew the eye on top of the head.

UNDERSIDE OF HEAD

With 4 mm (US 6) needles and CC2 cast on 3 sts. Work 5 rows in garter stitch, break yarn and hold the 3 sts on the needle. Rep from * to *, on the next row K the 3 sts you have been working, then K across the 3 held sts. (6 sts)

Next row: K2, K2tog, K2. (5 sts)

Next row: K2, K2tog, K1. (4 sts)

Work 4 rows in garter stitch. Change to MC and follow the head pattern from Row 1 to **. Cast off.

Sew the cast off edge to the WS of the scarf and join the two head pieces at the front in front of the tongue. Leave the side edges open to thread the scarf tail through.

Snake Mittens

These mittens have a long cuff to keep little arms warm. This is an easy pattern to follow if you want to practise knitting in the round. However, for an easier project, you can knit the mittens in one colour.

Size: 6–12 months (circumference up to 16 cm/6¼ in, length 20 cm/8 in); 12–18 months (circumference up to 17.5 cm/6¾ in, length 22 cm/8½ in). Sample shown is 6–12 months

Yarn: Sirdar Hayfield Bonus DK (100% acrylic; 100 g/3½ oz; 280 m/306 yd) MC grass green (shade 825) 50 g (2 oz); CC1 bright lemon yellow (shade 819) 25 g (1 oz); CC2 white (shade 961) 25 g (1 oz); CC3 classic red (shade 833) 25 g (1 oz)

Other materials: 4 buttons (6 mm/¼ in diameter)

Needles: 4 mm (US 6) dpns and straight needles

Tension: 10 cm (4 in) square = 22 sts x 28 rows in stocking stitch on 4 mm (US 6) needles with MC

Construction: Worked in the round

Skills needed: Working rib patterns, changing colours in the round

Knitting Pattern

MITTENS – MAKE 2

CUFF
With 4 mm (US 6) dpns and MC cast on 30(34) sts and join in the round.
Rnd 1: *K1, P1* to end of round.
Rnd 2: Join in CC1 and rep Rnd 1.
Rep Rnds 1 and 2 until piece measures 8.5(9.5) cm (3¼(3¾) in) long, ending with Rnd 2.
Next rnd: Rep Rnd 1.

MITTEN
Work all rem rnds with MC.
Rnd 1: K2(4), *M1, K5* 5 times, M1, K3(5). (36(40) sts)
K every rnd until piece measures 15.5(16.5) cm (6(6½) in). PM after st 18 (20).

> *Tip* When changing colours, keep the unused yarn at the wrong side of the work. Ensure any loose threads and buttons are securely fastened, as small pieces could be swallowed by young children.

MITTEN TOP

Rnd 1: K1, ssk, K to 3 sts before marker, K2tog, K1, sm, K1, ssk, K to last 3 sts, K2tog, K1. (32(36) sts)

Rnd 2: K.

Rep Rnds 1 and 2 until 12 sts remain.

Next rnd: Rep Rnd 1. (8 sts)

Break yarn, thread through and gather sts to cast off to finish the mitten.

EYES – MAKE 4

With 4 mm (US 6) straight needles and CC2 cast on 4 sts.

Row 1 and every alt row: [WS] P.

Row 2: [RS] Kfb, K to last st, kfb. (6 sts)

Row 4: Rep Row 2. (8 sts)

Row 6: Change to MC, K. (8 sts)

Row 8: K2tog, K to last 2 sts, K2tog. (6 sts)

Row 10: Rep Row 8. (4 sts)

Row 11: P.

Break yarn, thread through and gather sts to cast off. Sew running stitch around the edge of the knitted piece and pull the yarn to gather the stitches to form a small bobble with RS facing outward. Secure the yarn. Sew a small button on top. Sew two eyes on top of each mitten.

TONGUE – MAKE 2

With 4 mm (US 6) straight needles and CC3 cast on 10 sts using the cable cast on method (see page 118).

Row 1: Cast off 4 sts, K to end. (6 sts)

Row 2: Cast off 5 sts (1 st remains), cast on 3 sts. (4 sts)

Cast off all sts, weave in the yarn tails and sew the tongue to the underside of the mitten.

Swirly Snake Toy

A toy snake with a curled shape, made by working short rows along the body. This versatile snake can be wrapped around a crib or pram handle to provide little ones with hours of amusement.

Size: Approx. length 108 cm (42½ in), body is 6 cm (2½ in) wide

Yarn: Stylecraft Special Aran (100% acrylic; 100 g/3½ oz; 196 m/214 yd) MC meadow green (shade 1065) 100 g (3½ oz); CC1 aster blue (shade 1003) 50 g (2 oz); CC2 white (shade 1001) 50 g (2 oz); CC3 fondant pink (shade 1241) 50 g (2 oz)

Other materials: Approx. 150 g (6 oz) toy filling, 2 black buttons (10 mm/½ in diameter)

Needles: 4.5 mm (US 7) straight needles

Tension: 10 cm (4 in) square = 20 sts x 36 rows in stocking stitch on 4.5 mm (US 7) needles with MC

Construction: Worked flat

Skills needed: Knitting stripes, seaming, working short rows

Knitting Pattern

SNAKE – MAKE 1

With 4.5 mm (US 7) needles and MC cast on 20 sts.

Row 1 and every alt row: P.

Row 2: **K4, *M1, K1* 2 times, K4, rep from ** to end. (24 sts)

Row 4: **K5, *M1, K1* 2 times, K5, rep from ** to end. (28 sts)

Row 6: **K6, *M1, K1* 2 times, K6, rep from ** to end. (32 sts)

Row 8: **K7, *M1, K1* 2 times, K7, rep from ** to end. (36 sts)

Row 10: **K8, *M1, K1* 2 times, K8, rep from ** to end. (40 sts)

Rows 11 to 15: Starting and ending with a P row, work St st for 5 rows.

Row 16: *K7, K2tog, K1, K2tog tbl, K8, rep from * to end. (36 sts)

Row 18: *K6, K2tog, K1, K2tog tbl, K7, rep from * to end. (32 sts)

Row 20: *K5, K2tog, K1, K2tog tbl, K6, rep from * to end. (28 sts)

Row 22: *K4, K2tog, K1, K2tog tbl, K5, rep from * to end. (24 sts)

Row 24: *K5, K2tog, K5, rep from * to end. (22 sts)

Row 25 to 27: Starting and ending with a P row, work St st for 3 rows.

Row 28: K with CC.

Row 29: With CC, P19 w&t, K16 w&t, P14 w&t, K12 w&t, P17. (22 sts)

Rows 30 and 31: Rep Rows 28 and 29.

Row 32: Rep Row 28.

Row 33: P with CC. (22 sts)

Rows 34 and 35: With MC, starting with a K row, work St st for 2 rows. (22 sts)

Rep rows 28–35 fifteen times or to your desired length, alternating the CC in each set. I used the col sequence blue (CC1), white (CC2), pink (CC3).

TAIL

Work on the 22 sts on the needles with MC.

Rows 1–3: K.

Rows 4–6: P.

Row 7: *K3, K2tog, K1, K2tog tbl, K3* 2 times. (18 sts)

Row 8: K.

Row 9: *K2, K2tog, K1, K2tog tbl, K2* 2 times. (14 sts)

Rows 10 and 11: P.

Row 12: *P1, P2tog* 4 times, P2. (10 sts)

Row 13: K.

Row 14: *P2tog* 5 times. (5 sts)

Break yarn, thread through the sts and gather to cast off.

EYES – MAKE 2

With 4.5 mm (US 7) needles and CC2 cast on 4 sts.
Work Rows 1–6 in CC2 and the rem rows in MC.

Row 1: P.

Row 2: K1, M1, K to last st, M1, K1. (6 sts)

Rows 3 and 4: Rep Rows 1 and 2. (8 sts)

Rows 5 and 6: Starting with a P row, work in St st for 2 rows.

Rows 7–9: P.

Row 10: K.

Row 11: P2tog, P to last 2 sts, P2tog. (6 sts)

Row 12: K.

Row 13: *P2tog* 3 times. (3 sts)

Break yarn, thread through sts and gather to cast off. Sew a running stitch around the outside edge of the eye piece, add a piece of stuffing to the centre, then gather the stitches tightly to make a bobble eye. Sew buttons on to the front of the eyes.

TONGUE – MAKE 1

With 4.5 mm (US 7) and CC3 cast on 10 sts in CC3 using the cable cast on method (see page 118).

Row 1: Cast off the first 4 sts, K to end. (6 sts)

Row 2: Cast off the first 5 sts (1 st), cast on 3 sts using the cable cast on method. (4 sts)

Cast off all sts. Weave in the yarn tail, sewing the last cast off piece to the tongue to make a Y-shaped fork.

FINISHING

Sew the sides of the snake together from the tail to the head, adding stuffing as you sew. This seam lies on the bottom of the snake's body. Sew the cast on edges together to finish the mouth. Finish by sewing the tongue to the front of the mouth, and the eyes on the top of the head.

Crocodile Boots

These little boots use a picot cast off to add a crocodile-like texture to the cuff. The knitted I-cord ties will keep them on baby's feet, but you could replace this with a length of ribbon or a crochet chain.

Size: 6–12 months (length 11 cm/4½ in, width 7 cm/2¾ in); 12–18 months (length 12 cm/4¾ in, width 8 cm/3 in). Sample shown is 6–12 months

Yarn: Stylecraft Special Aran (100% acrylic; 100 g/3½ oz; 196 m/214 yd) MC meadow green (shade 1065) 50 g (2 oz); CC white (shade 1001) a small amount

Needles: 5 mm (US 8) straight needles, 2 x 4 mm (US 6) dpns

Tension: 10 cm (4 in) square = 18 sts x 24 rows in stocking stitch on 5 mm (US 8) needles with MC

Construction: Worked flat

Skills needed: Picot cast off, I-cord (see page 131)

Knitting Pattern

BOOTS – MAKE 2
With 5 mm (US 8) needles and MC cast on 32(36) sts.

SOLE
Row 1 and foll alt rows: K.
Row 2: *K1, M1, K14(16), M1, K1* 2 times. (36(40) sts)
Row 4: *K2, M1, K14(16), M1, K2* 2 times. (40(44) sts)
Row 6: *K3, M1, K14(16), M1, K3* 2 times. (44(48) sts)
Work 9(11) rows in garter stitch (K every row).

SHAPE FOOT
Row 1: K15(16), K2tog, K10(12), K2tog, K15(16). (42(46) sts)
Row 2 and foll alt rows: K.
Row 3: K15(16), K2tog, K8(10), K2tog, K15(16). (40(44) sts)
Row 5: K15(16), K2tog, K6(8), K2tog, K15(16). (38(42) sts)
Row 7: K15(16), K2tog, K4(6), K2tog, K15(16). (36(40) sts)
Row 9: K14(15), cast off next 8(10) sts, K rem sts. (28(30) sts)
Row 10: K across all sts. (28(30) sts)
Next rows: Work 6(8) rows in garter stitch. (28(30) sts)
Picot cast off all sts.

TIES – MAKE 2
Using 2 (4 mm/US 6) dpns work a 25 cm (10 in) I-cord on 3 sts. Cast off.

FINISHING
Sew the sole and back seams of the boot. Join the seam at the top of the boot (the cast off sts from Row 9). Thread the I-cord around the top of boot, weaving it in and out of the knitting, and tie at the centre front. Use CC to embroider vertical stitches around the front of each boot for the teeth.

Tip To work picot cast off, cast on 2 stitches using the cable cast on method (see page 118). Cast off four stitches, then pass the first stitch from the right-hand needle back over to the left-hand needle. Repeat to cast off all sts.

Crocodile Leg Warmers

These leg or arm warmers are a quick way to use up any leftover yarn from the crocodile stole. They are knitted in the round and the pattern is easy to adjust to the size you need.

Size: 3–9 months (circumference up to 18 cm/7 in); 9–12 months (circumference up to 20 cm/8 in); 12–24 months (circumference up to 22 cm/8½ in). Sample shown is 3–9 months

Yarn: Stylecraft Special Chunky (100% acrylic; 100 g/3½ oz; 144 m/157 yd) MC meadow green (shade 1065) 50 g (2 oz); CC lemon yellow (shade 1020) 50 g (2 oz)

Needles: 6.5 mm (US 10.5) dpns

Tension: 10 cm (4 in) square = 13 sts x 18 rows in stocking stitch on 6.5 mm (US 10.5) needles with MC

Construction: Worked in the round

Skills needed: Knitting stripes in the round

Knitting Pattern

LEG WARMERS – MAKE 2

With 6.5 mm (US 10.5) needles and MC cast on 22(24,26) stitches and join in the round.

Rnds 1 to 6: *K1, P1* to end of rnd.

Rnd 7: With MC, K, PM at end of rnd. (22 sts)

For the next 22(26, 30) rnds K 2 rnds in CC foll by 2 rnds in MC, ending with 2 rnds in CC.

Next rnd: with MC K.

Next 6 rnds: with MC, *K1, P1* to end of round.

Cast off loosely and weave in yarn tails to finish.

Crocodile Stole

This pattern uses cable knitting to make the scales on the crocodile's back. The legs and striped lining for the tummy are optional, and you can adapt the pattern to your chosen length – but remember you may need more yarn if you do this.

Size: width 13 cm (5 in) at widest point, length 81 cm (32 in)

Yarn: Stylecraft Special Chunky (100% acrylic; 100 g/3½ oz; 144 m/157 yd) MC meadow green (shade 1065) 100 g/3½ oz; CC1 lemon yellow (shade 1020) 50 g (2 oz); CC2 white (shade 1001) 15 g (¾ oz)

Other materials: 2 buttons (11 mm/½ in diameter) and a small amount of toy filling

Needles: 6 mm (US 10) straight needles, and 2 x 6 mm (US 10) dpns, cable needle

Notions: Stitch holders

Tension: 10 cm (4 in) square = 14 sts x 20 rows in stocking stitch on 6 mm (US 10) needles with MC

Construction: Worked flat

Skills needed: Cable knitting, making an I-cord, knitting stripes

Knitting Pattern

STOLE FRONT – MAKE 1

HEAD AND BODY
With 6 mm (US 10) straight needles and MC cast on 12 sts.
Row 1: [WS] P.
Row 2: [RS] K1, M1, K to last st, M1, K1. (14 sts)
Rows 3–5: Starting and ending with a P row, work St st for 3 rows.
Rows 6–21: Rep Rows 2–5 four times. (22 sts)
Rows 22–31: Starting with a K row, work in St st. ** (22 sts)
Row 32: K7, C4B, C4F, K7.
Row 33, 35, and 37: P.
Row 34: K5, C4B, K4, C4F, K5.
Row 36: K3, C4B, K8, C4F, K3.
Rep Rows 32–37 nineteen times, until you have reached your desired scarf length minus 12 cm (4¾ in). Mark the ends of the last row before working the tail.

> *Tips*
> ◆ C4B means cable four back: work to the position of the C4B. Slip the next 2 sts on to a cable needle and hold at the back of the work. Knit the next 2 sts on the LH needle, then knit the 2 sts from the cable needle.
>
> ◆ C4F means cable four front: work to the position of the C4F. Slip the next 2 sts on to a cable needle and hold at the front of the work. Knit the next 2 sts on the LH needle, then knit the 2 sts from the cable needle.

TAIL

Row 1: [RS] Ssk, K5, C4B, C4F, K5, K2tog. (20 sts)
Row 2 and all foll WS rows: [WS] P.
Row 3: K4, C4B, K4, C4F, K4.
Row 5: Ssk, K4, C4B, C4F, K4, K2tog. (18 sts)
Row 7: K3, C4B, K4, C4F, K3.
Row 9: Ssk, K3, C4B, C4F, K3, K2tog. (16 sts)
Row 11: K2, C4B, K4, C4F, K2.
Row 13: Ssk, K to last 2 sts, K2tog. (14 sts)
Rep Row 13 on all rem RS rows until 2 sts remain. Cast off.

SCARF LINING – MAKE 1

HEAD AND BODY

In MC work as for head to **.
Row 32: Ssk, K to last 2 sts, K2tog. (20 sts)
Row 33: P.
Row 34: Rep Row 32. (18 sts)
Starting with a P row, work in St st in stripe sequence of 2 rows CC1 then 2 rows MC for the rest of the pattern. Work until the lining is the same length to the row markers as the top piece, then work tail.

TAIL

Row 1: [RS] Ssk, K to last 2 sts, K2tog. (16 sts)
Row 2 and all foll WS rows: [WS] P.
Rows 3, 5, and 7: K.
Row 9: Ssk, K to last 2 sts, K2tog. (14 sts)
Rows 11 and 13: K.
Row 15: Ssk, K to last 2 sts, K2tog. (12 sts)
Rep row 15 on all rem RS rows until 2 sts remain. Cast off.
Sew the lining piece to the top piece around the edges. With white yarn embroider vertical stitches around the mouth for the teeth.

LEGS – MAKE 4

Make 4 legs per stole and 3 toes per leg.

TOES – MAKE 12

With 6 mm (US 10) straight needles and MC cast on 3 sts.

Row 1: [RS] *Kfb* 2 times, turn. (5 sts)

Rows 2 and 4: P4.

Row 3: K4, turn.

Row 5: *K2tog* 2 times, K1. (3 sts)

Using 2 (6 mm/US 10) dpns, and with the RS facing you, work an I-cord on these 3 sts for 6 rows, then break yarn and transfer the sts to a stitch holder.

LEGS – MAKE 4

Transfer 3 toe pieces to a 6 mm (US 10) straight needle with the RS facing you. (9 sts)

Row 1: *K2tog* 2 times, K1, *K2tog* 2 times. (5 sts)

Using 2 (6 mm/US 10) dpns, and with the RS facing you, work an I-cord on these 5 sts for 6 rows. Then, with the WS facing you and using straight 6 mm (US 10) needles, work the legs.

Next row: [WS] P.

Next row: [RS] K1, M1, K to last st, M1, K1. (7 sts)

Rep these 2 rows to inc to 11 sts, then cast off. Sew the cast off edge to the side of the body.

EYES – MAKE 2

With 6 mm (US 10) straight needles and CC2 cast on 4 sts. Work Rows 1–6 in CC2 and rem rows in MC.

Row 1: P.

Row 2: K1, M1, K to last st, M1, K1. (6 sts)

Rows 3 and 4: Rep Rows 1 and 2. (8 sts)

Rows 5 and 6: Starting with a P row, work in St st for 2 rows.

Rows 7–9: P.

Rows 10 and 12: K.

Row 11: P2tog, P to last 2 sts, P2tog. (6 sts)

Row 13: *P2tog* 3 times. (3 sts)

Break yarn, thread through sts and gather to cast off. Sew a running stitch around the outside edge of the eye piece, add a piece of stuffing to the centre, then gather the stitches tightly to make a bobble eye. Sew a button on to the front of the eye and sew the finished eyes to the top of the crocodile's head.

NOSTRILS – MAKE 2

With 6 mm (US 10) straight needles and MC cast on 8 sts.

Row 1: K.

Row 2: *K2tog* to end of row. (4 sts)

Break yarn, thread through sts and gather to cast off. Sew the side edges together to make a small cone. Sew the finished nostrils to the top of the head.

Tortoise Storage Baskets

Use these stacking storage baskets to hold cotton wool and other essentials in the nursery. Knitted in super chunky yarn, they are quick to knit and take just one skein of yarn. You can make these baskets wider or taller, you will just need some more yarn to do so. The tortoise head and feet are made separately and sewn on, so you can make the baskets without decoration if you prefer.

Size: small (height 7 cm/2¾ in, diameter 12 cm/4¾ in); large (height 7 cm/2¾ in, diameter 15 cm/6 in)

Yarn: Lion Brand Hometown USA Super Chunky (100% acrylic; 100 g/3½ oz; 54 m/64 yd); Sirdar Hayfield Bonus DK (100% acrylic; 100 g/3½ oz; 280 m/306 yd)

Purple turtle: MC Lion Brand mardi gras red multi (shade 203) 100 g (3½ oz); CC1 Sirdar powder blue (shade 960) 50 g (2 oz); CC2 Sirdar white (shade 961) 50 g (2 oz)

Yellow turtle: MC Lion Brand ducks yellow and green (shade 135) 100 g (3½ oz); CC1 Sirdar sunflower yellow (shade 978) 50 g (2 oz); CC2 Sirdar white (shade 961) 50 g (2 oz)

Other materials: approx. 50 g (2 oz) toy filling, 2 buttons (6 mm/¼ in diameter) for each basket

Needles: 4 mm (US 6) and 10 mm (US 15) straight needles

Tension: 10 cm (4 in) square = 8 sts x 10 rows in stocking stitch on 10 mm (US 15) needles in MC

Construction: Worked flat

Skills needed: Decreases and increases, seaming

Knitting Pattern

LARGE BASKET – MAKE 1

With MC and 10 mm (US 15) needles cast on 6 sts.
Row 1: *Kfb* 6 times. (12 sts)
Rows 2, 4, 6, 8, and 10: K.
Row 3: *Kfb, K1* 6 times. (18 sts)
Row 5: *Kfb, K2* 6 times. (24 sts)
Row 7: *Kfb, K3* 6 times. (30 sts)
Row 9: *Kfb, K4* 6 times. (36 sts)
Row 11: *Kfb, K5* 6 times. (42 sts)
Starting with a P row, work in St st for 9 rows. Cast off.

Tips
- To knit these baskets in the round, cast on using dpns and follow the pattern except P rnds 2, 4, 6, 8 and 10.
- To make a wider basket, cont incs in sets of 6 sts from Row 11 to the desired width.
- To make a taller basket, add extra rows before casting off.

SMALL BASKET – MAKE 1

Work Rows 1 to 7 as for large basket. (30 sts).
Starting with a P row, work 7 rows St st. Cast off.

FINISHING

Sew the side edges together and weave in yarn tails. Note that the right side of the basket is the reverse stocking side.

TORTOISE FEET – MAKE 4 FOR EACH BASKET

With CC1 and 4 mm (US 6) needles cast on 24 sts.
Rows 1 to 11: Starting with a P row, work in St st.
Row 12: [RS] *K2tog, K1* 8 times. (16 sts)
Row 13: P.
Row 14: *K2tog* 8 times. (8 sts)
Break yarn, thread through the sts and gather to cast off. Sew the side edges and stuff the foot. Gather the cast on sts and pull tightly to make a small ball, and sew this edge to the side of the basket.

HEAD – MAKE 1 FOR EACH BASKET

With CC1 and 4 mm (US 6) needles cast on 33 sts.
Rows 1 to 15: Starting with a P row, work in St st.
Row 16: [RS] *K2tog, K1* 11 times. (22 sts)
Row 17: P.
Row 18: *K2tog* 11 times. (11 sts)
Gather sts and finish in the same way as the feet.

EYES – MAKE 2 FOR EACH BASKET

With MC and 4 mm (US 6) needles cast on 6 sts. Work Rows 1–4 with CC1 and Rows 5–9 with CC2
Row 1: [WS] P.
Row 2: Kfb, K to last st, kfb. (8 sts)
Rows 3 and 4: Rep Rows 1 and 2. (10 sts)
Row 5: P.
Row 6: K2tog, K to last 2 sts, K2tog. (8 sts)
Rows 7 and 8: Rep Rows 5 and 6. (6 sts)
Row 9: P.
Break yarn, thread through sts and gather to cast off. Using the yarn tail, sew a running stitch around the outside edge of the knitted piece, add a little stuffing to the centre and pull the yarn to gather and make a small bobble. Sew a 6 mm (¼ in) button on to the front of each eye, and sew the eyes on top of the head.

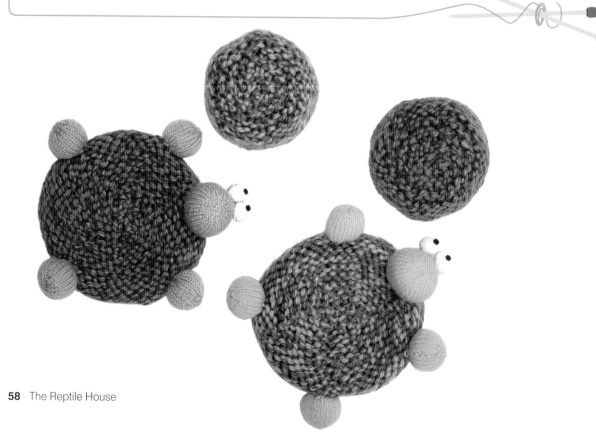

Frog Hat

A fun and cosy hat with frog toe ear flaps to tie under the chin and 'googly' stuffed frog eyes for a touch of playful embellishment.

Size: 6–24 months (stretches to fit head circumference 36–44 cm/14–17¼ in)

Yarn: Stylecraft Special Chunky (100% acrylic; 100 g/3½ oz; 144 m/157 yd) MC aspen green (shade 1422) 100 g (3½ oz); CC white (shade 1001) 10 g (½ oz)

Other materials: 2 buttons (11 mm/½ in diameter) and small amount of toy filling

Needles: 6 mm (US 10) dpns and straight needles

Notions: Stitch holder

Tension: 10 cm (4 in) square = 14 sts x 20 rows in stocking stitch on 6 mm (US 10) needles with MC

Construction: Hat is worked in the round; eyes and ear flaps are worked flat

Skills needed: Working in the round, seaming, making I-cord (see page 131)

Knitting Pattern

EAR FLAPS – MAKE 2
Make 3 toes per ear flap and make 2 ear flaps per hat; work the toe bobble flat on 6 mm (US 10) straight needles.

TOES – MAKE 3 FOR EACH EAR FLAP
With MC and 6 mm (US 10) straight needles cast on 3 sts.
Row 1: [RS] *kfb* 2 times, turn. (5 sts)
Row 2: P4.
Row 3: K4, turn.
Row 4: P4.
Row 5: *K2tog* 2 times, K1. (3 sts)
Using 2 x 6mm (US 10) dpns, and with the RS facing you, work I-cord on these 3 sts for 6 rows, then break yarn and hold the sts.

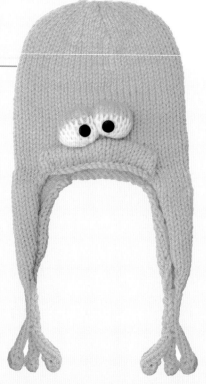

LEG

Place the three toe pieces on a straight 6 mm (US 10) needle with the RS facing you. (9 sts)

Row 1: *K2tog* 2 times, K1, *K2tog* 2 times. (5 sts)

Using 2 (6 mm/US 10) dpns, and with the RS facing you, work an I-cord on these 5 sts for 6 rows. Then, with the WS facing you and using straight 6 mm (US 10) needles, work the rest of the ear flap flat.

FLAP

Row 1: [WS] P.

Row 2: K1, M1, K to last st, M1, K1. (7 sts)

Rep these 2 rows until you have 15 sts.

Starting and ending with a P row, work St st until the piece is 20 cm (8 in) long.

For the first ear flap, break yarn and keep the sts on the needle.

Repeat to make the second ear flap, but do not break the yarn.

Next row: K15 sts for the flap from the needle, cast on 16 sts at the end of the row for the brim, K the 15 held sts from the first ear flap, then cast on 11 sts for the back of the hat. (57 sts).

HAT – MAKE 1

Join the 57 sts in the round.

Rnd 1: K14 across second ear flap, K2tog, K14 for brim, K2tog, K13 for first ear flap, K2tog, K10 for back, PM. (54 sts).

K all rnds until the hat is 15 cm (6 in) high.

SHAPE TOP

Rnd 1: *K2tog, K4* 9 times. (45 sts)

Rnds 2 and 3: K.

Rnd 4: *K2tog, K3* 9 times. (36 sts)

Rnds 5 and 6: K.

Rnd 7: *K2tog, K2* 9 times. (27 sts)

Rnd 8: *K2tog, K1* 9 times. (18 sts)

Rnd 9: *K2tog* 9 times. (9 sts)

Break yarn, thread through sts and gather to cast off.

BRIM – MAKE 1

With MC and 6 mm (US 10) straight needles cast on 19 sts.

Starting with a K row, work 4 rows in St st.

Row 5: Ssk, K to last 2 sts, K2tog. (17 sts)

Row 6: P.

Row 7: Rep Row 5. (15 sts)

Cast off. Stitch the cast on edge to the brim of the hat and sew the cast off edge on to the hat front.

EYES – MAKE 2

With MC and 6 mm (US 10) straight needles cast on 7 sts.

Work Rows 1–4 in MC, and Rows 5–9 in CC.

Row 1 and all alt rows: P.

Row 2: Kfbf, K to last st, kfbf. (11 sts)

Rows 4 and 6: K

Row 8: K3tog, K to last 3 sts, K3tog. (7 sts)

Break yarn, thread through sts and gather to cast off. Using the tail of yarn, sew a running stitch around the outside edge of the knitted piece and pull the yarn to gather into a bobble, adding a little stuffing. Secure the thread. Sew a button on to the eye and sew the eyes to the front of the hat above the brim.

Tip To work kfbf, knit into the front, then the back, then the front again of the next stitch to make 2 additional stitches.

Chapter 4

Polar Regions

Chilly polar climates call for snuggly paw print booties and mittens, and cute animal headbands to keep little ears warm. Let it snow!

Arctic Headbands

Use these easy-to-knit headbands to practise knitting textured stitch patterns. You can choose to embellish them with polar bear, wolf or Arctic hare ears. Choose your own combination of stitch pattern and ears.

Size: approx. 5 cm (2 in) wide. Suggested lengths: newborns 33–36 cm (13–14 in); 3–6 months 36–43 cm (14–17 in); 6–12 months 41–45 cm (16–18 in); 12–36 months 43–48 cm (17–19 in)

Yarn: Bear and Wolf headbands: Rowan British Sheep Breeds Chunky Undyed (100% wool; 100 g/3½ oz; 110 m/120 yd) MC blue faced Leicester (shade 950) 50 g (2 oz). Arctic Hare headband: Stylecraft Special Chunky (100% acrylic; 100 g/3½ oz; 144 m/157 yd) MC parchment beige (shade 1218) 50 g (2 oz)

Needles: 5.5 mm (US 9) straight needles

Tension: 10 cm (4 in) square = 15 sts x 40 rows in garter stitch on 5.5 mm (US 9) needles with MC

Construction: Worked flat

Skills needed: Textured and ribbed stitch patterns

Knitting Pattern

HEADBAND – MAKE 1

RIBBED STITCH PATTERN

With MC and 5.5 mm (US 9) needles cast on 9 sts.
Row 1: [WS] K2, P5, K1 sl1 pwise wyif.
Rows 2 and 3: Rep Row 1.
Row 4: K to last st, sl1 pwise wyif.
Rows 5 and 6: Rep Row 4.
Rep Rows 1–6 until you reach the desired length. Cast off and sew the short ends together.

RICK RACK RIB

With MC and 5.5 mm (US 9) needles cast on 10 sts.
Row 1: [RS] Sl1 pwise wyif, K2, P1, ktwist, P1, K3.
Row 2: [WS] Sl1 pwise wyif, K1, P1, K1, ptwist, K1, P1, K2.
Rep Rows 1 and 2 until you reach the desired length. Cast off and sew the short ends together.

SEED STITCH

With MC and 5.5 mm (US 9) straight needles cast on 9 sts.
Row 1: K3, *P1, K1* 2 times, K1, sl1 pwise wyif.
Rep Row 1 until you reach the desired length. Cast off and sew the short ends together.

Tips
- ◆ To work ktwist, take the RH needle behind the 1st st on the LH needle and K into the back of the 2nd st on the LH needle, K the 1st st, then slip both sts off the LH needle.
- ◆ To work ptwist, wyif skip the 1st st on the LH needle and P into the 2nd st on the LH needle, P the 1st st, then slip both sts off the LH needle.

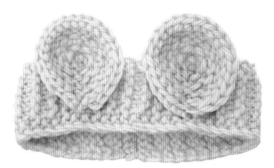

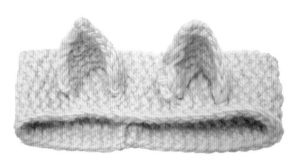

POLAR BEAR EARS – MAKE 2

With MC and 5.5 mm (US 9) straight needles cast on 3 sts.
Row 1: *Kfb* 3 times. (6 sts)
Rows 2, 4, 6, and 8: K.
Row 3: *Kfb* 6 times. (12 sts)
Row 5: *Kfb, K1* 6 times. (18 sts)
Row 7: *Kfb, K2* 6 times. (24 sts)
Cast off. Sew the side edges to the top of the headband in a semicircle
(the cast off edge is the outer edge of the ear).

WOLF EARS – MAKE 2

With MC and 5.5 mm (US 9) straight needles cast on 14 sts.
Row 1: Sl1 pwise, K to last 2 sts, K2tog. (13 sts)
Rep Row 1 until 2 sts rem.
Foll row: Sl1, K1, psso. (1 st)
Cast off. Fold the ear lengthways and stitch the cast on edge
to the headband.

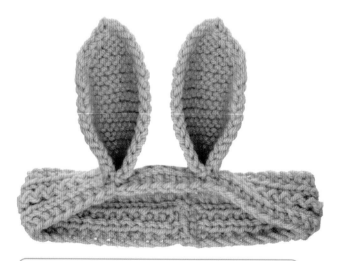

ARCTIC HARE EARS – MAKE 2

With MC and 5.5 mm (US 9) straight needles cast on 14 sts and
work 20 rows in garter stitch (K every row).
Then follow Wolf Ears pattern from Row 1 to cast off and make up as
for the Wolf Ears.

Polar Bear Paw Print Shoes and Mittens

These little shoes with paw prints on the sole have their own matching mittens. Snowflake yarn can be difficult to work with, so keep your stitches fairly loose – you may find it easier to use metal needles. The yarn does not stretch as much as regular yarn, so the cuff for the mittens is worked in an Aran yarn. As an alternative, you could knit these in a chunky yarn, and if the knitted circles are too difficult, you can sew felt circles for paw prints instead.

Size: Shoes: 0–3 months (length 10 cm/ 4 in, width 6 cm/2½ in); 3–6 months (length 11.5 cm/4½ in, width 7 cm/2¾ in); 6–12 months (length 13 cm/5 in, width 8 cm/3 in). Samples shown are 6–12 months (brown) and 0–3 months (white). Mittens: one size (length 12 cm/4¾ in, width 8 cm/3 in).

Yarn: Sirdar Snuggly Snowflake Chunky (100% polyester; 25 g/1 oz; 62 m/68 yd) MC creamy white (shade 0631) 25 g (1 oz); CC1 Patons Wool Blend Aran (wool mix; 100 g/3½ oz; 185 m/202 yd) cream (shade 002) 20 g (¾ oz); CC2 Sirdar Hayfield Bonus DK (100% acrylic; 100 g/3½ oz; 280 m/306 yd) black (shade 965) 20 g (¾ oz)

Other materials: 2 buttons (13 mm/½ in diameter), 2 small snap fasteners

Needles: 5.5 mm (US 9) and 3.75 mm (US 5) straight needles, 2 x 5 mm (US 8) dpns

Tension: 10 cm (4 in) square = 14 sts x 28 rows in garter stitch on 5.5 mm (US 9) needles in garter stitch with MC

Construction: Worked flat

Skills needed: Seaming, casting on stitches at the beginning of a row, making an I-cord (see page 131)

Knitting Pattern

RIGHT SHOE – MAKE 1

With MC and 5.5 mm (US 9) needles cast on 20(24,28) sts.
Row 1 and every alt row: [WS] K.
Row 2: [RS] *Kfb, K8(10,12), kfb* 2 times. (24(28,32) sts)
Row 4: *K1, kfb, K8(10,12), kfb, K1* 2 times. (28(32,36) sts)
Row 6: K2, *kfb, K8(10,12), kfb*, K1, kfb 2 times, K1, rep from * to *, K2. (34(38,42) sts)
Work 5(7,9) rows in garter stitch.

TOP OF RIGHT SHOE

Row 1: K8(10,12), ssk 4 times, K2, K2tog 4 times, K8(10,12). (26(30,34) sts)
Row 2: K6(7,8) [group A], cast off 14(16,18) sts, K rem sts [group B]. (12(14,16) sts) ***
Row 3: K6(7,8) sts [group B], turn leaving group A sts unworked.
Row 4: Using cable cast on, cast on 12(14,16) sts at beg of row, then K all sts. (18(21,24) sts)
Cast off, then work on the group A sts with RS facing you.
Next 3 rows: K. (6(7,8) sts)
Cast off. Sew the sole and back seam of the shoe, sew snap fasteners to the end of the strap and side of shoe, and add a small button on top of the strap to decorate.

LEFT SHOE – MAKE 1

Foll the right shoe pattern to ***
Next 3 rows: K [group B]. (6 (7, 8) sts)
Cast off, then work on the group A sts with RS facing you.
Next 2 rows: K. (6(7,8) sts)
Foll row: Rep top of right shoe pattern Row 4. (18 (21,24) sts)
Cast off and finish as for right shoe.

MITTENS – MAKE 2

With CC1 and 5.5 mm (US 9) needles cast on 22 sts.
Row 1: [RS] *K1,P1* to end.
Rows 2 to 6: Rep Row 1.
Change to MC and work garter stitch until knitted piece is 10 cm (4 in) long ending with a WS row.

SHAPE MITTEN TOP

Row 1: [RS] K1, ssk, K5, K2tog, K1, ssk, K6, K2tog, K1. (18 sts)
Row 2 and foll alt rows: K.
Row 3: K1, ssk, K3, K2tog, K1, ssk, K4, K2tog, K1. (14 sts)
Row 5: *K2tog* to end of row. (7 sts)
Break yarn, thread through sts and gather to cast off the top of the mitten. Sew side seams.

MITTEN LOOP

With CC1 and 2 (5 mm/US 8) dpns cast on 4 sts and work an I-cord until you have an 8 cm (3 in) length. Cast off. Sew the ends of the I-cord to the top of the mitten.

PAW PRINTS – MAKE 2 LARGE AND 6 SMALL

LARGE PAD

With CC2 and 3.75 mm (US 5) needles cast on 7 sts.
Row 1: *Kfb* to end of row. (14 sts)
Rows 2 and 4: K.
Row 3: *Kfb, K1* to end of row. (21 sts)
Row 5: *Kfb, K2* to end of row. (28 sts)
Cast off all sts loosely. Gather cast on sts together and join side edges to form a circle. Sew on to sole of shoe or front of mitten.

SMALL PAD

Work as for large pad pattern but work Row 1 only, then cast off all sts loosely and finish as for large pad.
Sew the paw prints on to each shoe or mitten.

Tips
◆ The mittens can be made larger or smaller by increasing/decreasing the number of cast on sts in increments of 4 sts and altering length and shaping sts as needed.

◆ To work the paw pad circles in the round, cast on to dpns and join in the round and follow pattern except purl the even numbered rnds.

Penguin Baby Bottle Carrier and Toy

This little penguin is a cute way to carry baby bottles, and the matching toy follows the same basic pattern. The penguins are knitted flat, but can easily be converted to knitting in the round if you prefer. Use a machine washable yarn for the carrier to make it easy to clean up any spills.

Size: approx. 9 cm (3½ in) diameter and 13 cm (5 in) high

Yarn: King Cole Big Value DK (100% acrylic; 100 g/3½ oz; 290 m/317 yd) MC black (shade 048) 50 g (2 oz); CC1 white (shade 001) 50 g (2 oz); CC2 gold yellow (shade 055) 50 g (2 oz)

Other materials: 2 buttons (6 mm/¼ in diameter), small white felt circles, 100 g (3½ oz) of toy filling

Needles: 4 mm (US 6) straight needles, 2 x 4 mm (US 6) dpns

Tension: 10 cm (4 in) square = 22 sts x 28 rows in stocking stitch on 4 mm (US 6) needles with MC

Construction: Worked flat

Skills needed: Changing colours, seaming, making I-cord (see page 131)

Knitting Pattern

PENGUIN CARRIER

BODY – MAKE 1

With 4 mm (US 6) needles and CC1 cast on 9 sts.
Row 1 and every alt (odd numbered) row: [WS] P.
Row 2: [RS] K1, *kfb* 8 times. (17 sts)
Row 4: K1, *kfb, K1* 8 times. (25 sts)
Row 6: K1, *kfb, K2* 8 times. (33 sts)
Row 8: K1, *kfb, K3* 8 times. (41 sts)
Row 10: K1, *kfb, K4* 8 times. (49 sts)
Rows 11–29: Starting and ending with a P row work in St st for 19 rows.
Rows 30–47: Change to MC and starting with a K row, work 18 rows in St st
Cast off loosely. Gather cast on stitches at base and sew side edges together.

> *Tip* To convert to working in the round, for the body, cast on 9 sts and arrange on 3 dpns. For Rnd 1 and every odd-numbered rnd K. For even numbered rnds follow the pattern for body. To make the toy, add filling before casting off.

Knitting Pattern

EYES AND BEAK – MAKE 1

With 4 mm (US 6) needles and CC1 cast on 7 sts.
Row 1 and every alt row: P.
Row 2: K1, M1, K to last st, M1, K1. (9 sts)
Rows 4 and 6: Rep Row 2. (13 sts)
Rows 8 and 10: K.
Row 12: K1, k2tog tbl, K to last 3 sts, k2tog, K1. (11 sts)
Change to CC2.
Row 13 and every alt row: P.
Rows 14, 16, and 18: Rep Row 12. (5 sts)
Row 20: K1, K3tog, K1. (3 sts)
Break yarn, thread through sts and gather to cast off. Sew the finished eye piece on to the front of the carrier and sew small buttons on top of small white circles of felt fabric for eyes.

WINGS – MAKE 2

With 4 mm (US 6) needles and MC cast on 11 sts.
Row 1: K1, kfb, K to last 3 sts, K2tog, K1. (11 sts)
Row 2: K.
Rows 3–12: Rep Rows 1 and 2.
Cast off and sew wings to the sides of the penguin.

CADDY STRAP – MAKE 1

With 1 (4 mm/US 6) dpn and MC cast on 4 sts. Using 2 dpns, work a 40 cm (15¾ in) I-cord. Cast off. Sew each end to opposite sides of the top of the carrier.

PENGUIN FEET – MAKE 2

With 4 mm (US 6) needles and CC2 cast on 7 sts.
Row 1: K.
Row 2: K to last 2 sts, K2tog. (6 sts)
Rep Row 2 until 3 sts rem. Cast off and sew feet to the underside of the penguin.

PENGUIN TOY

BODY

Work as for carrier pattern to Row 47.
Row 48: K1, *K2tog, K4* 8 times. (41 sts)
Row 49 and all foll alt rows: P.
Row 50: K1, *K2tog, K3* 8 times. (33 sts)
Row 52: K1, *K2tog, K2* 8 times. (25 sts)
Row 54: K1, *K2tog, K1* 8 times. (17 sts)
Row 56: K1, *K2tog* 8 times. (9 sts)
Break yarn, thread through sts and gather to cast off the top of the head. Sew the side edges together, adding stuffing, and finish by gathering the cast on sts at the base. Add some strands to top of head to make hair and trim to desired length.

WINGS

Work as for carrier pattern.

BEAK

Work as for carrier pattern.

FEET

Work as for carrier pattern.

> **Tip** To cast off the carrier top loosely: k2tog then slip the new stitch on the right needle back to the left needle. Repeat until all stitches are cast off. This gives a nice stretchy edge that will slide over the bottle.

Penguin Mittens

These mittens will keep hands warm, but the garter stitch texture will also make these super bathtime wash mitts for bigger kids! The coloured panel is knitted using intarsia colourwork, with the blocks of colour worked with separate bobbins of yarn. Use a machine washable acrylic yarn to prevent shrinking.

Size: Stretches to fit hand circumference 18 cm (7 in), length 18 cm (7 in)

Yarn: King Cole Big Value DK (100% acrylic; 100 g/3½ oz; 290 m/317 yd); MC black (shade 048) 50 g (2 oz); CC1 white (shade 001) 50 g (2 oz); CC2 gold yellow (shade 055) 50 g (2 oz)

Other materials: 2 buttons (6 mm/¼ in diameter)

Needles: 4 mm (US 6) and 3.75 mm (US 5) straight needles

Notions: Darning or tapestry needle, stitch holder

Tension: 10 cm (4 in) square = 22 sts x 28 rows in stocking stitch on 4 mm (US 6) needles with MC

Construction: Worked flat

Skills: Intarsia colourwork

Knitting Pattern

RIGHT MITTEN – MAKE 1

CUFF
With 4 mm (US 6) needles and MC cast on 34 sts.
Joining in CC1 as required work as follows:
Row 1: [RS] MC K5, CC1 K9, MC K20.
Row 2: [WS] MC K20, CC1 K9, MC K5.
Rep Rows 1 and 2 until piece measures 6 cm (2½ in), ending with a WS row.

SHAPE THUMB
Row 1: [RS] MC K5, CC1 K9, MC K3, M1, K2, M1, K15. (36 sts)
Rows 2, 4, 6, 8, 10, and 12: [WS] MC K to last 14 sts, CC1 K9, MC K5.
Row 3: MC K5, CC1 K9, MC K3, M1, K4, M1, K15. (38 sts)
Row 5: MC K5, CC1 K9, MC K3, M1, K6, M1, K15. (40 sts)
Row 7: MC K5, CC1 K9, MC K3, M1, K8, M1, K15. (42 sts)
Row 9: MC K5, CC1 K9, MC K3, M1, K10, M1, K15. (44 sts)
Row 11: MC K5, CC1 K9, MC K5.
Row 13: MC K5, CC1 K9, MC K3, slip next 12 sts on to a stitch holder for thumb, MC K15. (32 sts)

HAND

Row 1: [WS] MC K18, CC1 K9, MC K5. (32 sts)
Row 2: [RS] MC K5, CC1 K9, MC K18.
Rep Rows 1 and 2 until mitten measures 15 cm (6 in) long, ending with a WS row.

SHAPE TOP

Work all rem rows in MC.
Rows 1 and 2: K. (32 sts) PM after 16th st.
Row 3: K1, ssk, K to 2 sts before marker, K2tog, slip marker, ssk, K to last 3 sts, K2tog, K1. (28 sts)
Row 4 and all foll alt rows: K.
Rows 5, 7, 9, and 11: Rep Row 3. (12 sts)
Row 13: *K2tog* to end of row. (6 sts)
Break yarn, thread through sts and gather to cast off to close the top of the mitten.

THUMB

Transfer the 12 sts from the stitch holder to a 4 mm (US 6) needle with RS facing you.
With MC work 14 rows in garter stitch.
Row 15: *K2tog* to end of row (6 sts).
Break the yarn and finish as for the top of the mitten.

FINISHING

Sew side edges together and add strands of MC to the top of the mitten for the penguin's fuzzy hair.

LEFT MITTEN – MAKE 1

CUFF

With 4 mm (US 6) needles and MC cast on 34 sts.
Row 1: [RS] MC K20, CC1 K9, MC K5.
Row 2: [WS] MC K5, CC1 K9, MC K20.
Rep Rows 1 and 2 until piece measures 6 cm (2½ in), ending with a WS row.

SHAPE THUMB

Row 1: [RS] MC K15, M1, K2, M1, K3, CC1 K9, MC K5. (36 sts)
Rows 2, 4, 6, 8, 10, and 12: [WS] MC K5, CC1 K9, MC K rem sts.
Row 3: MC K15, M1, K4, M1, K3, CC1 K9, MC K5. (38 sts)
Row 5: MC K15, M1, K6, M1, K3, CC1 K9, MC K5. (40 sts)
Row 7: MC K15, M1, K8, M1, K3, CC1 K9, MC K5. (42 sts)
Row 9: MC K15, M1, K10, M1, K3, CC1 K9, MC K5. (44 sts)
Row 11: MC K30, CC1 K9, MC K5.
Row 13: MC K15, slip next 12 sts on to a stitch holder for thumb, MC K3, CC1 K9, MC K5. (32 sts)

HAND

Row 1: [WS] MC K5, CC1 K9, MC K18. (32 sts)
Row 2: [RS] MC K18, CC1 K9, MC K5.
Rep Rows 1 and 2 until the mitten measures 15 cm (6 in) long, ending with a WS row.
Shape the top, work the thumb and finish as for the right mitten.

EYES – MAKE 4

With 3.75 mm (US 5) needles and CC1 cast on 7 sts.
Row 1: *Kfb* to end of row. (14 sts)
Cast off all sts loosely. Sew sides together and gather cast on sts to make a small circle, then sew to the top of the mittens. Sew a small button on to each circle for the pupil.

BEAK – MAKE 2

With 4 mm (US 6) needles and CC2 cast on 7 sts.
Row 1: K.
Row 2: K to last 2 sts, K2tog. (6 sts)
Rep Row 2 until 2 sts rem.
Foll row: Sl1, K1, psso. (1 st)
Cast off and stitch to the mitten under the eyes.

FEET – MAKE 4

Work as for beak until 3 sts rem. Cast off and stitch to the bottom cuff of the mitten.

Chapter 5

Tropical Seas

The tropical seas are bright and colourful.
Make an easy-to-knit aquatic bib, create
some fun fish or explore the waves with
a tropical chevron blanket.

Under-the-Sea Bib

This is a simple bib, ideal for beginner knitters. It is knitted in garter stitch (see page 121), with the little fish motif knitted separately. The bigger bib size is ideal for toddlers, but you can make this bib smaller simply by casting on fewer stitches and adjusting the number of rows. If working the buttonhole seems too tricky, simply knit all the stitches on these rows and sew a press stud on to the bib and strap instead.

Size: 23 cm (9 in) wide, 28 cm (11 in) long (excluding strap)

Yarn: Stylecraft Special Chunky (100% acrylic; 100 g/3½ oz; 144 m/157 yd) MC aster blue (shade 1003) 100 g (3½ oz); Sirdar Hayfield Bonus DK (100% acrylic; 100 g/3½ oz; 280 m/306 yd); CC sunflower yellow (shade 978) 10 g (½ oz)

Other materials: 1 large button (3.5 cm/1¼ in diameter), 1 small button (6 mm/¼ in diameter), small white felt circle

Needles: 6 mm (US 10) and 4 mm (US 6) straight needles

Tension: 10 cm (4 in) square = 14 sts x 28 rows in garter stitch on 6 mm (US 10) needles with MC

Construction: Worked flat

Skills needed: Knit stitch, casting on and casting off

Knitting Pattern

BIB
With 6 mm (US 10) needles and MC cast on 37 sts.
Row 1: K.
Rep Row 1 until the bib measures 27.5 cm (10¾ in) long.
Cast off 28 sts, K to end. (9 sts)
Foll row: K. (9 sts)
Work these 9 sts in garter stitch until the strap meaures 30 cm (12 in) long.
Foll row: K3, cast off 3 sts for buttonhole, K3. (6 sts)
Foll row: K3, cast on 3 sts, K3. (9 sts)
Foll row: K.
Rep the last row for 2 cm (¾ in), then cast off. Weave in yarn tails and sew large button under the strap at the top of the bib.

FISH
With 4 mm (US 6) needles and CC cast on 28 sts.
Step 1: Cast off 4 sts, slip the st from the right to left needle. (24 sts)
Step 2: Using cable cast on method, cast on 4 sts. (28 sts)
Step 3: Cast off 4 sts, slip the st on the right needle to the left needle. (24 sts)

BODY
Row 1: *K2tog, K2* to end of row. (18 sts)
Rows 2 and 4: K.
Row 3: *K2tog, K1* to end of row. (12 sts)
Row 5: *K2tog* to end of row. (6 sts)
Break yarn, thread through sts and gather to cast off and close the centre of the body. Sew the side edges together to make a circular shape. Sew the small button on top of a white felt circle on to the fish for the eye. Stitch on to the finished bib.

Tropical Fish Toys

These little fish make super toys on their own or you could make several and hang them on lengths of yarn or ribbon for a baby mobile.

Size: 12 cm (4¾ in) wide, 11 cm (4½ in) high

Yarn: Sirdar Hayfield Bonus DK (100% acrylic; 100 g/3½ oz; 280 m/306 yd) MC bright orange (shade 981) or sunflower yellow (shade 978) 50 g (2 oz); CC white (shade 961) 50 g (2 oz); King Cole Cottonsoft DK (100% cotton; 100 g/3½ oz; 210 m/229 yd); MC mint green (shade 715) 50 g (2 oz)

Other materials: 50 g (2 oz) toy filling and 2 buttons (6 mm/¼ in diameter) for each fish

Needles: 4 mm (US 6) straight needles

Tension: 10 cm (4 in) square = 22 sts x 28 rows stocking stitch on 4 mm (US 6) needles with MC

Construction: Worked flat

Skills needed: Knit one purl one rib, decreases and increases, knitting stripes, seaming

Knitting Pattern

BODY – MAKE 1

With MC and 4 mm (US 6) needles cast on 26 sts.
Rows 1–9: *K1, P1, rep from * to end. (26 sts)
Row 10: [WS] *P2tog* 13 times. (13 sts)
Row 11: K1, *kfb, K1, rep from * to end. (19 sts)
Row 12 and every foll alt row: P.
Row 13: K1, *kfb, K3, kfb, K2, kfb, K1, rep from * to end. (25 sts)
Row 15: K1, *kfb, K4, kfb, K4, kfb, K1, rep from * to end. (31 sts)
Row 17: K1, *kfb, K12, kfb, K1, rep from * to end. (35 sts)
Work Rows 18,19, 22, 23, 26, and 27 in CC, and work rem rows in MC.
Rows 18–34: Starting with a P row, work in St st
Row 35: K1, *K2tog, K5, K2tog, K5, K2tog, K1, rep from * to end. (29 sts)
Row 36 and every foll alt row: P.
Row 37: K1, *K2tog, K4, K2tog, K3, K2tog, K1, rep from * to end. (23 sts)
Row 39: K1, *K2tog, K2, K2tog, K2, K2tog, K1, rep from * to end. (17 sts)
Row 41: K1, *K2tog, K1* 5 times, K1. (12 sts)
Row 43: *K2tog* 6 times. (6 sts)
Break yarn, thread through sts and gather to cast off and close the nose of the fish. Sew side edges together (this seam runs down underside of fish). Stuff the fish through the cast on edge, then sew cast on edges together at end of tail. To define tail, sew a running stitch around Row 10, pull yarn to gather knitting and secure the thread.

FIN – MAKE 2

With MC and 4 mm (US 6) needles cast on 14 sts.

Row 1: *K1, P1*, rep to end.

Rows 2–13: Rep Row 1 (or until the piece is square).

Cast off. Fold the piece in half diagonally to make a triangle, sew together open edges. Sew a fin to the top and bottom of the fish.

EYES – MAKE 2

With CC and 4 mm (US 6) needles cast on 4 sts.

Row 1: [WS] P.

Row 2: [RS] Kfb, K to last st, kfb. (6 sts)

Rows 3 and 4: Rep Rows 1 and 2. (8 sts)

Row 5: P.

Row 6: K2tog, K to last 2 sts, K2tog. (6 sts)

Rows 7 and 8: Rep Rows 5 and 6. (4 sts)

Break yarn, thread through sts and gather to cast off. Using the yarn tail, sew a running stitch around the outside edge of the piece, add a little stuffing to the centre, then pull the yarn to gather the sts to make a small bobble and secure the thread. Sew a small button to the front for the pupil and sew a finished eye to each side of the fish.

Sea Turtle Coasters

These little turtles will brighten up the nursery and they also make fun toys (minus buttons). You can knit the shell flat or in the round – instructions are given for both.

Knitting Pattern

SHELL – MAKE 1

TO WORK IN THE ROUND

With CC and 6 mm (US 10) dpns cast on 42 sts using the continental cast on method (see page 119) and join in the round.

Rnd 1 and every alt. rnd: P.
Rnd 2: *K2tog, K5* 6 times. (36 sts)
Rnd 4: *K2tog, K4* 6 times. (30 sts)
Rnd 6: *K2tog, K3* 6 times. (24 sts)
Rnd 8: *K2tog, K2* 6 times. (18 sts)
Rnd 10: *K2tog, K1* 6 times. (12 sts)
Rnd 12: *K2tog* 6 times. (6 sts)

Break yarn, thread through sts and gather to cast off the centre of the shell. Secure the thread and weave in the tail.

TO WORK FLAT

With CC and 6 mm (US 10) straight needles cast on 42 sts using the continental cast on method (see page 119). Foll the pattern as for working in the round, but K all odd-numbered rows. Finish as for the working in the round pattern, then sew the side edges together to finish the shell.

COLOURWORK

For the blue and yellow turtle, cast on with MC and work rest of pattern with CC. For the pink and purple striped turtle, cast on with CC, then work 2 rows/rnds in MC and 2 rows/rnds in CC and rep these 4 rows/rnds.

HEAD – MAKE 1

With MC and 6 mm (US 10) straight needles cast on 20 sts using continental cast on.
Rows 1 and 3: K.
Row 2: K4, *K2tog* 6 times, K4. (14 sts)
Row 4: K1, *K2tog* 6 times, K1. (8 sts)

Divide the sts between 2 needles, with 4 sts on each needle, and graft the live sts together using kitchener stitch to join the seam down the centre of the head. Sew the side edge of the head to one side of the shell. Sew the buttons on to white felt circles for eyes and sew to the top of the head.

Yarn: Stylecraft Special Chunky (100% acrylic; 100 g/3½ oz; 144 m/157 yd); pink and purple turtle MC fondant pink (shade 1241) 1 oz (25 g), CC lavender purple (shade 1188) 1 oz (25 g); blue and yellow turtle MC aster blue (shade 1003) 1 oz (25 g), CC lemon yellow (shade 1020) 1 oz (25 g); green and yellow turtle MC lemon yellow (shade 1020) 1 oz (25 g) CC aspen green (shade 1422) 1 oz (25 g)

Other materials: 2 buttons (6 mm/¼ in diameter), small white felt circles

Needles: 6 mm (US 10) straight needles and dpns

Tension: 10 cm (4 in) square = 14 sts x 20 rows in stocking stitch on 6 mm (US 10) needles with MC

Construction: Worked flat or in the round

Skills needed: Seaming, grafting live stitches together, changing colours, working in the round (if desired)

FEET – MAKE 4

With MC and 6 mm (US 10) straight needles cast on 12 sts.
Row 1: K.
Row 2: *K2tog* 6 times. (6 sts)

Break yarn, thread through sts and gather to cast off. Form piece into a semicircle with cast on sts as outside edge and sew side edge to the edge of the shell.

Tropical Waves Baby Blanket

This baby blanket uses increases and decreases to make a chevron waves pattern. Experiment with different widths of stripes or colours to create your own waves design. You can make the blanket wider or narrower by increasing or decreasing the number of cast-on stitches in multiples of 17.

Size: 55 x 61 cm (21½ x 24 in)

Yarn: Stylecraft Special Chunky (100% acrylic; 100 g/3½ oz; 144 m/157 yd) MC white (shade 1001) 200 g (7 oz); CC1 aster blue (shade 1003) 100 g (3½ oz); CC2 baby blue (shade 1232) 100 g (3½ oz); CC3 lemon yellow (shade 1020) 100 g (3½ oz)

Needles: 6 mm (US 10) 80 cm (32 in) circular needle

Tension: 10 cm (4 in) square = 14 sts x 28 rows in garter stitch on 6 mm (US 10) needles in MC

Construction: Worked flat on circular needles to accommodate the number of stitches

Skills needed: Increases and decreases, picking up stitches

Knitting Pattern

BLANKET
With MC and 6 mm (US 10) circular needles cast on 104 sts.
Rows 1 and 2: K.
Row 3: K1 *kfb, K6, sl1 pwise, K2tog, psso, K6, kfb, rep from * to last st, K1. (104 sts)
Rep rows 2 and 3 in colour sequence: CC1, MC, CC2, MC, CC3, MC (two rows in each colour), until the blanket measures 60 cm (21½ in) long at shortest point, ending on Rows 2 and 3 with MC.
Foll row: With MC K.
Cast off and weave in the yarn tails.

SIDE BORDERS
With MC and 6 mm (US 10) circular needles, pick up one st per garter stitch ridge along one side edge of the blanket.
Rows 1, 2, and 3: K2tog, K to last 2 sts, K2tog.
Cast off.
Repeat on the other side edge.

Shark Bodywarmer

This bodywarmer has a surprise on the hood – teeth! It is worked flat on a circular needle to accommodate stitches and the armholes are worked in the round.

Size: 6–12 months (chest 44–46 cm/17¼–18 in); 12–18 months (chest 47–49 cm/18½–19¼ in); 18–24 months (chest 50–52cm/19¾–20½ in). Sample shown is 6–12 months

Yarn: King Cole Big Value Chunky (100% acrylic; 100 g/3½ oz; 152 m/166 yd) MC grey (shade 547) 200(250) g (7(9) oz); Stylecraft Special Chunky (100% acrylic; 100 g/3½ oz; 144 m/157 yd) CC white (shade 1001) 50 g (2 oz)

Other materials: 5 front buttons (13 mm/¾ in diameter), 2 eye buttons (13 mm/¾ in diameter), 2 felt circles

Needles: 6 mm (US 10) straight needles, 40 cm (15 in) circular needle and dpns

Notions: 2 stitch holders

Tension: 10 cm (4 in) square = 14 sts x 20 rows in stocking stitch on 6 mm (US) needles with MC

Construction: Working flat on circular needles, working in the round

Skills needed: Holding live stitches and grafting, intarsia colourwork

Knitting Pattern

BODYWARMER

NOTE ON WORKING THE BUTTONHOLES
Work first buttonholes on Row 4 for girls/Row 3 for boys, and then every 14th row above that before the hood as follows: work on start of RS row for girls/start of WS row for boys. Instead of knitting the first 4 sts work *K1, yo, K2tog, K1* then foll pattern for the rest of the row.

BODY
With MC and 6 mm (US 10) circular needle cast on 70(74,78) sts.
Row 1: [WS] K4, *P2, K2* to last 6 sts, P2, K4.
Row 2: [RS] K4, *K2, P2* to last 6 sts, K6.
Rows 3 and 4: Rep Rows 1 and 2.
Row 5: K4, P to last 4 sts, K4.
Row 6: K.
Rep Rows 5 and 6 until piece measures 18(20,22) cm (7(8,8½) in), ending with a WS row.
Next RS row: K18(19,20), cast off the next 2 sts for armhole, K to last 20(21,22) sts, cast off the next 2 sts for armhole, K rem sts (66(70,74) sts).

LEFT FRONT
Work on the first 18(19,20) sts for left front only with WS facing you. Hold rem sts on a stitch holder to work later for the right front and back.
Row 1: [WS] K4, P to armhole, turn.
Row 2: [RS] K1, ssk, K rem sts. (17(18,19) sts)
Rows 3 and 4: Rep Rows 1 and 2. (16(17,18) sts)
Row 5: Rep Row 1.
Row 6: K16(17,18).
Rep Rows 5 and 6 until the knitted piece measures 30(32,34) cm (12(12½,13½) in) long, ending with a RS row.
Next WS row: Cast off first 5(5,6) sts, P rem sts (11(12,12) sts). Hold these 11(12,12) sts on a stitch holder for the hood.

BACK

Return the held 30(32,34) sts for back to the needles with WS facing you.

Row 1: P to armhole. (30(32,34) sts)

Row 2: K1, ssk, K to last 3 sts, K2tog, K1. (28(30,32) sts)

Rows 3 and 4: Rep Rows 1 and 2. (26(28,30) sts)

Starting with a P row work in St st until the knitted piece measures 30(32,34) cm (12(12½,13½) in) long, ending with a RS row. Next WS row: Cast off the first and last 5(5,6) sts, P the centre sts (16(18,18) sts). Hold these 16(18,18) sts on a stitch holder for the hood.

RIGHT FRONT

Return the held 18(19,20) sts for the right front to the needles with WS facing you.

Row 1: P to last 4 sts, K4.

Row 2: K to last 3 sts, K2tog, K1. (17(18,19) sts)

Rows 3 and 4: Rep Rows 1 and 2. (16(17,18) sts)

Row 5: Rep Row 1.

Row 6: K16(17,18).

Rep Rows 5 and 6 until the knitted piece measures 30(32,34) cm (12(12½,13½) in) long, ending with a RS row.

Next WS row: P to last 5(5,6) sts, cast off the last 5(5,6) sts. Hold the remaining 11(12,12) sts on a stitch holder for the hood.

HOOD

Place the held 38(42,42) sts for the hood on a 6 mm (US 10) circular needle with RS facing you.

Row 1: [RS] With MC K4(6,6),* kfb, K4* to last 4(6,6) sts, K rem sts. (44(48,48) sts). PM after 22nd(24th, 24th) stitch (centre back).

Row 2: [WS] With MC K4, P to last 4 sts, K4.

Row 3: Work teeth at border. With CC kfb, K1, kfb; with MC K to 1 st before centre marker, M1, K1, sm, K1, M1, K to last 3 sts, in CC kfb, K1, kfb.

Row 4: With CC K5, with MC K1, P to last 6 sts, K1, with CC K5.

Row 5: With CC kfb, K3, kfb, with MC K to 1 st before centre marker, M1, K1, sm, K1, M1, K to last 5 sts, with CC, kfb, K3, kfb.

Row 6: With CC K7, with MC K1, P to last 8 sts, K1, with CC K7.

Row 7: With CC kfb, K5, kfb, with MC K to 1 st before centre marker, M1, K1, sm, K1, M1, K to last 7 sts, with CC, kfb, K5, kfb.

Row 8: With CC K9, with MC K1, P to last 10 sts, K1, with CC K9.

Row 9: With CC kfb, K7, kfb, with MC K to 1 st before centre marker, M1, K1, sm, K1, M1, K to last 9 sts, pm, with CC kfb, K7, kfb.

Row 10: With CC cast off 8 sts, K to 1st marker and remove, with MC K1, P to last 12 sts, K1, with CC K3, cast off last 8 sts.

Rep Rows 3–10 five times, with six teeth on each side of the hood border (you can make a taller hood if desired). Divide the sts equally on to two needles and graft together to close the seam at the top of the hood. Sew buttons on to white felt circles and on to the top of the hood for eyes, and sew buttons on to the front placket under the buttonholes.

ARMHOLES

Sew together the shoulder seams, joining the cast off sts from the front pieces to the back. With RS facing you, with MC and starting at the bottom of one armhole, use 6 mm (US 10) dpns to pick up approx. 3 sts every 4 rows and 2 sts at underarm around the armhole. The total no. of sts should be a multiple of 4. Join in the round.

Rnds 1 to 5: *K2, p2* to end of rnd.

Cast off loosely and weave in yarn tails.

Chapter 6

In the Forest

The forest comes to life with these beautiful woodland wildlife projects, including a useful baby bib, a decorative owl pillow and some cosy winter knits.

Fox Bib

This practical bib uses chevron knitting to create the fox's head with eye detail for a bit of fun.

Knitting Pattern

BIB
With CC2 and 4 mm (US 6) needles cast on 61 sts.
Row 1: [RS] K.
Row 2: [WS] K1, kfb, K26, K2tog, K1, ssk, K to last 2 sts, kfb, K1. (61 sts)
Rep Rows 1 and 2 until piece measures 6 cm (2½ in), ending with a WS row.
Next RS row: Change to CC1 and rep Rows 1 and 2 until piece measures 9.5 cm (3¾ in) ending with a WS row.
From next RS row: Change to MC and rep Rows 1 and 2 three times.

SHAPE TOP OF HEAD
Cont with MC.
Row 1 and all foll alt rows: K.
Row 2: K1, kfb, K25, K2tog, K3, ssk, K to last 2 sts, kfb, K1.
Row 4: K1, kfb, K24, K2tog, K5, ssk, K to last 2 sts, kfb, K1.
Row 6: K1, kfb, K23, K2tog, K7, ssk, K to last 2 sts, kfb, K1.
Row 8: K1, kfb, K22, K2tog, K9, ssk, K to last 2 sts, kfb, K1.
Row 10: K1, kfb, K21, K2tog, K11, ssk, K to last 2 sts, kfb, K1.
Row 12: K1, kfb, K20, K2tog, K13, ssk, K to last 2 sts, kfb, K1.
Row 14: K1, kfb, K19, K2tog, K15, ssk, K to last 2 sts, kfb, K1.
Row 16: K1, kfb, K18, K2tog, K17, ssk, K to last 2 sts, kfb, K1.
Row 18: K1, kfb, K17, K2tog, K19, ssk, K to last 2 sts, kfb, K1.
Row 20: K1, kfb, K16, K2tog, K21, ssk, K to last 2 sts, kfb, K1.
Row 22: K1, kfb, K15, K2tog, K23, ssk, K to last 2 sts, kfb, K1.
Row 24: K1, kfb, K14, K2tog, K25, ssk, K to last 2 sts, kfb, K1.
Rows 26 and 28: rep Row 24.
Row 29: K.
Cast off.

STRAP 1
With MC and 4 mm (US 6) needles cast on 5 sts.
Row 1 and foll alt rows: K.
Row 2: K1, kfb, K to last 2 sts, kfb, K1. (7 sts)
Rows 4 and 6: Rep Row 2. (11 sts)
Foll rows: K until strap measures 14 cm (5½ in).
Cast off.

Size: 21 cm (8 ¼ in) wide x 30 cm (12 in high (from ears to chin)

Yarn: Sirdar Hayfield Bonus DK (100% acrylic; 100 g/3½ oz; 280 m/306 yd); MC fox orange (shade 779) 50 g (2 oz); CC1 white (shade 961) 50 g (2 oz); CC2 rusty orange (shade 780) 50 g (2 oz)

Other materials: 1 fastening button (13 mm/¾ in diameter), 2 eye buttons (13 mm/ ¾ in diameter) or circles of black felt, circles of white felt for eyes, black felt for nose

Needles: 4 mm (US 6) straight needles

Tension: 10 cm (4 in) square = 22 sts x 40 rows in garter stitch on 4 mm (US 6) needles with MC

Construction: Worked flat

Skills needed: Changing colours at the end of a row, increases and decreases

STRAP 2
With CC1 and 4 mm (US 6) needles cast on 2 sts.
Row 1 and foll alt rows: K.
Row 2: Kfb, K1. (3 sts)
Row 4: *Kfb* 2 times, K1. (5 sts)
Row 6: Kfb, K to last 2 sts, kfb, K1. (7 sts)
Rows 8 and 10: Rep Row 6. (11 sts)
Row 12: K5, yo, K2tog, K rem sts. (11 sts)
Row 14: Rep Row 6. (13 sts)
Rows 15 to 23: K.
Row 24: K1, ssk, K to last 3 sts, K2tog, K1. (11 sts)
Foll rows: Change to MC and K until strap measures 15 cm (6 in). Cast off.

FINISHING
Sew the cast off edges of the straps under the ears of the bib and sew a button on the end of Strap 1. Sew the eyes and nose on to the front.

Owl Pillow

This colourful owl-shaped pillow will cheer up any nursery or sofa. Use Fair Isle or stranded colourwork to create the pattern on the owl's tummy. If this sounds too tricky, you could knit the tummy (Rows 1 to 39) in one colour or work in stripes.

Size: approx. 33 x 30 cm (13 x 12 in)

Yarn: Stylecraft Special Chunky (100% acrylic; 100 g/3½ oz; 144 m/157 yd) MC meadow green (shade 1065) 100 g (3½ oz); CC1 lavender purple (shade 1188) 50 g (2 oz); CC2 fondant pink (shade 1241) 50 g (2 oz); CC3 white (shade 1001) 50 g (2 oz); CC4 lemon yellow (shade 1020) 50 g (2 oz)

Other materials: 200 g (7 oz) toy filling, 2 x 15 mm (¾ in) diameter buttons

Needles: 5 mm (US 8) straight needles

Tension: 10 cm (4 in) square = 16 sts x 22 rows in stocking stitch on 5 mm (US 8) needles with MC

Construction: Worked flat

Skills: Fair Isle stranded colourwork, seaming

Knitting Pattern

BODY – MAKE 2

With CC1 and 5 mm (US 8) needles cast on 35 sts.
Row 1: P. (35 sts)
Row 2: Kfb, K to last st, kfb. (37 sts)
Join in CC2 and work as follows:
Row 3: CC1 P4,* CC2 P1, CC1 P3, rep from * to last st, CC1 P1. (37 sts)
Row 4: CC1 kfb, K2, * CC2 K3, CC1 K1, rep from * to last 2 sts, CC1 K1, kfb. (39 sts)
Row 5: CC1 P5, * CC2 P1, CC1 P3, rep from * to last 2 sts, CC1 P2. (39 sts)
Row 6: CC1 kfb, K2, * CC2 K1, CC1 K3, rep from * to last 4 sts, CC2 K1, CC1 K2, kfb. (41 sts)
Row 7: CC1 P3,* CC2 P3, CC1 P1, rep from * to last 2 sts, CC1 P2. (41 sts)
Row 8: CC1 kfb, K3, * CC2 K1, CC1 K3, rep from * to last st, CC1 kfb. (43 sts)
Row 9: * CC1 P3, CC2 P1, rep from * to last 3 sts, CC1 P3. (43 sts)
Row 10: CC1 K2, * CC2 K3, CC1 K1, rep from * to last st, CC1 K1. (43 sts)
Row 11: Rep Row 9.
Row 12: CC1 K5, * CC2 K1, CC1 K3, rep from * to last 2 sts, CC1 K2. (43 sts)
Row 13: CC1 P4, * CC2 P3, CC1 P1, rep from * to last 3 sts, CC1 P3. (43 sts)
Row 14: Rep Row 12.
Rows 15–38: Rep Rows 9–14 four times.
Row 39: CC1 P. (43 sts)
Rows 40–55: Work all rem rows in MC.
Starting with a K row work St st for 16 rows.
Row 56: K2tog tbl, K to last 2 sts, K2tog. (41 sts)
Rows 57–59: Starting with a P row work St st for 3 rows.
Rows 60–67: Rep Rows 56–59 twice. (37 sts)
Row 68: Kfb, K to last st, kfb. (39 sts)
Row 69: P.
Rows 70–73: Rep Rows 68 and 69 twice. (43 sts)
Row 74: Rep Row 68. (45 sts)

Cast off. Sew the body pieces together around the edges, adding stuffing as you sew.

BEAK – MAKE 1

With CC4 and 5 mm (US 8) needles cast on 5 sts.

Row 1 and all foll alt rows: P.
Row 2: K2, M1, K1, M1, K2. (7 sts)
Row 4: K3, M1, K1, M1, K3. (9 sts)
Row 6: K4, M1, K1, M1, K4. (11 sts)
Row 8: K3, ssk, K1, K2tog, K3. (9 sts)
Row 10: K2, ssk, K1, K2tog, K2. (7 sts)
Row 12: K1, ssk, K1, K2tog, K1. (5 sts)
Row 14: K1, K3tog, K1. (3 sts)
Break yarn, thread through sts and gather to cast off. Sew the beak to the front of the owl.

EYES – MAKE 2

With CC3 and 5 mm (US 8) needles cast on 6 sts.
Work Rows 1–11 with CC3 and rows 12–21 with MC.

Row 1 and every alt row: P.
Row 2: Kfbf, K to last st, kfbf. (10 sts)
Rows 4 and 6: Kfb, K to last st, kfb. (14 sts)
Rows 8 and 12: K.
Row 10: Rep Row 4. (16 sts)
Rows 14, 16, and 18: K2tog tbl, K to last 2 sts, K2tog. (10 sts)
Row 20: K3tog tbl, K to last 3 sts, K3tog. (6 sts)
Cast off. Sew a black button on to each eye piece and stitch the eyes on to the front of the owl above the beak, adding a little stuffing underneath to pad them.

Tip
To work kfbf, knit into the front, then the back, then the front again of the next stitch to make 2 additional stitches.

WINGS – MAKE 2

With MC and 5 mm (US 8) needles cast on 17 sts.

Row 1 and all foll alt rows: P.
Row 2: K8, M1, K1, M1, K8. (19 sts)
Row 4: K9, M1, K1, M1, K9. (21 sts)
Row 6: K10, M1, K1, M1, K10. (23 sts)
Rows 8, 10, 12, 14, and 16: Cont incs as per rows 2, 4 and 6, inc by 2 sts per row. (33 sts)
Row 18: K14, ssk, K1, K2tog, K14. (31 sts)
Row 20: K13, ssk, K1, K2tog, K13. (29 sts)
Rows 22, 24, and 26: Cont decs as per rows 18 and 20, dec by 2 sts per row. (23 sts)
Row 28: K2tog, K7, ssk, K1, K2tog, K7, ssk. (19 sts)
Row 30: K2tog, K5, ssk, K1, K2tog, K5, ssk. (15 sts)
Row 32: K2tog, K3, ssk, K1, K2tog, K3, ssk. (11 sts)
Row 34: K2tog, K1, ssk, K1, K2tog, K1, ssk. (7 sts)
Row 36: K1, K2tog, K1, ssk, K1. (5 sts)
Row 38: K1, K3tog, K1. (3 sts)
Break yarn, thread through sts and gather to cast off. Sew the wings to the sides of the owl so that the cast on edge of the wing lines up with Row 40 of the body. Add stuffing underneath the wings to pad them out.

Reindeer Antler Hat

This little beanie hat is an easy knit, and for some extra fun you can add antlers to the top of the hat. You can substitute the antlers with the bear, wolf or hare ears from the polar bear, wolf or Arctic hare headband patterns.

Size: 12–36 months (stretches to fit head circumference 46 cm/18 in, height 20 cm/ 8 in)

Yarn: Stylecraft Special Chunky (100% acrylic; 100 g/3½ oz; 144 m/157 yd) MC parchment beige (shade 1218) 100 g (3½ oz); CC raspberry pink (shade 1023) 100 g (3½ oz)

Other materials: handful of toy filling

Needles: 5.5 mm (US 9) and 6 mm (US 10) straight needles

Notions: darning or tapestry needle, stitch holders

Tension: 10 cm (4 in) square = 14 sts x 20 rows in stocking stitch on 6 mm (US 10) needles with MC

Construction: Worked flat

Skills needed: Seaming, knitting stripes, holding stitches.

Knitting Pattern

HAT – MAKE 1
With MC and 5.5 mm (US 9) needles cast on 62 sts.

BRIM
Row 1: *K2, P2* to last 2 sts, K2.
Row 2: *P2, K2* to last 2 sts, P2.
Rep Rows 1 and 2 twice.

HAT
Foll row: Switch to 6 mm (US 10) needles and K.
Foll rows: Starting and ending with a P row, work in stripes of 2 rows CC then 2 rows MC, and rep pattern in St st until piece measures 15 cm (6 in).

> **Tip**
> To make a smaller hat, knit in Aran wool on 5 mm (US 8) needles. To convert the hat pattern to knitting in the round, cast on 2 sts fewer. Work the brim in K2, P2 rib for six rounds, and for the hat K all rnds in stripe pattern. To shape, ignore the first K2 sts for rnds 1, 5, 7, 9 and 11 (you do not need to work these) and K the alt rnds.

SHAPE TOP

Work rem rows with MC.

Row 1: [RS] K2,*K2tog, K4* to end. (52 sts)

Rows 2 to 4: Starting and ending with a P row, work in St st.

Row 5: K2,*K2tog, K3* to end. (42 sts)

Row 6 and all foll WS rows: P.

Row 7: K2,*K2tog, K2* to end. (32 sts)

Row 9: K2,*K2tog, K1* to end. (22 sts)

Row 11: *K2tog* to end of row. (11 sts)

Break yarn, thread through sts and gather to cast off the top of the hat. Sew the side edges together and weave in yarn tails to finish.

ANTLERS – MAKE 2

With CC and size 6 mm (US 10) needles cast on 12 sts.

Row 1 and every alt (odd numbered) row: P.

Row 2: K5, M1, K2, M1, K5. (14 sts)

Row 4: K5, M1, K4, M1, K5. (16 sts)

Row 6: K5, M1, K6, M1, K5. (18 sts)

Row 8: K5, M1, K8, M1, K5. (20 sts)

Row 10: K5, M1, K10, M1, K5. (22 sts)

Row 12: K6, slip 10 sts on to a stitch holder (bottom antler branch), K6. (12 sts)

Row 14: K. (12 sts)

Rows 16–22: Rep Rows 2–8. (20 sts)

Row 24: K5, slip 10 sts on to a stitch holder (top antler branch), K5. (10 sts)

Rows 26 and 28: K. (10 sts)

Row 30: *K2tog* 5 times. (5 sts)

Break yarn, thread through sts and gather to cast off the tip of the antlers. Secure the thread.

TOP ANTLER

Transfer the 10 held sts to the knitting needle with RS facing you. Starting with a K row, work St st for 4 rows.

Foll row: *K2tog* 5 times. (5 sts)

Break yarn and gather sts as for the antler.

BOTTOM ANTLER

Transfer the 10 held sts to the knitting needle with RS facing you. Starting with a K row, work St st for 6 rows.

Foll row: *K2tog* 5 times. (5 sts)

Break yarn and gather sts as for the antler.

Sew the side edges of the antlers together, add toy filling and sew the cast on edge to the top of the hat.

Robin Mittens

These little fingerless mittens have a flip top and a robin embellishment. They can be made with or without stripes in the two different designs shown.

Knitting Pattern

LEFT MITTEN

CUFF
With MC and 4 mm (US 6) needles cast on 34(36,38) sts. Work in K1, P1 rib for 5(5.5,6) cm (2(2¼,2½) in).

SHAPE THUMB
Row 1 and all foll alt rows: [WS] P.
Row 2: [RS] K15(16,17), M1, K2, M1, K17(18,19). (36(38,40) sts)
Row 4: K15(16,17), M1, K4, M1, K17(18,19). (38(40,42) sts)
Row 6: K15(16,17), M1, K6, M1, K17(18,19). (40(42,44) sts)
Row 8: K15(16,17), M1, K8, M1, K17(18,19). (42(44,46) sts)
Row 10: K15(16,17), M1, K10, M1, K17(18,19). (44(46,48) sts)
smallest size: work 2 rows St st
medium and large sizes: Add another inc row to (48,50) sts, then work (3,5) rows St st
Next RS row: K15(16,17), slip 12(14,14) sts on to stitch holder, K17(18,19). (32(34,36) sts)

MITTEN TOP
Work in St st until mitten measures 12.5(15,17.5) cm (5(6,6¾) in) long. Cast off loosely.

THUMB TOP
Place the 12(14,14) sts from the holder on to the knitting needle with RS facing you and work St st for 5(6,8) rows. Cast off loosely.

> **Tip** As a pattern variation, work the cuff in CC and the mitten in stripes of 2 rows MC followed by 2 rows CC as shown on the left.

Size: 12–18 months (hand circumference 16 cm/6¼ in); 18–36 months (hand circumference 17 cm/6¾ in); 36 months and older (hand circumference 18 cm/7 in)

Yarn: Sirdar Country Style DK (40% nylon, 30% wool, 30% acrylic; 50 g/2 oz; 155 m/ 170 yd) MC mink brown (shade 477) 50 g (2 oz). Rowan Pure Wool DK (100% wool; 50 g/2 oz; 125 m/137 yd) CC kiss red (shade 036) 1 oz (25 g)

Other materials: 4 small buttons for eyes (6 mm/¼ in diameter), white felt circles, small amount of yellow yarn, 2 medium red buttons (13 mm/¾ in diameter)

Needles: 4 mm (US 6) straight needles

Notions: stitch holder

Tension: 10 cm (4 in) square = 22 sts x 28 rows in stocking stitch on 4 mm (US 6) needles with MC

Construction: Worked flat

Skills needed: Holding live stitches, seaming

FLIP TOP

Make the button loop. With MC and 4 mm (US 6) needles cast on 11 sts, then cast off 10 sts (1 st). Cast on 6(7,8) sts. (7(8,9) sts)

Row 1 and every alt odd numbered row: [WS] P.

Row 2: *Kfb* to end of row. (14(16,18) sts)

Row 4: *K1, kfb, K3(4,5), kfb, K1, rep from * to end. (18(20,22) sts)

Row 6: * K1, kfb, K5(6,7), kfb, K1, rep from * to end. (22(24,26) sts)

Row 8: * K1, kfb, K7(8,9), kfb, K1, rep from * to end. (26(28,30) sts)

Row 10: * K1, kfb, K9(10,11), kfb, K1, rep from * to end. (30(32,34) sts)

Row 12: K1, kfb, K14(15,16), kfb, K rem sts. (32(34,36) sts). Starting with a P row, work in St st until piece measures 7.5(⅞,8.5) cm (3(3¼,3½) in). Cast off.

ROBIN TUMMY

With CC and 4 mm (US 6) needles cast on 24 sts.

Row 1: [RS] *K2tog, K1* 8 times. (16 sts)

Row 2: K.

Row 3: *K2tog* 8 times. (8 sts)

Break yarn, thread through sts and gather to cast off the tummy. Sew side seams to make a circle.

RIGHT MITTEN

CUFF

Work as for left mitten.

SHAPE THUMB

Row 1 and all foll alt rows: [WS] P.

Row 2: [RS] K17(18,19), M1, K2, M1, K15(16,17). (36(38,40) sts)

Row 4: K17(18,19), M1, K4, M1, K15(16,17). (38(40,42) sts)

Row 6: K17(18,19), M1, K6, M1, K15(16,17). (40(42,44) sts)

Row 8: K17(18,19), M1, K8, M1, K15(16,17). (42(44,46) sts)

Row 10: K17(18,19), M1, K10, M1, K15(16,17). (44(46,48) sts)

smallest size: Work 2 rows St st

medium and large sizes: Add another inc row to (48,50) sts. Work (3,5) rows in St st

Next RS row: K17(18,19), slip 12(14,14) sts on to stitch holder, K15(16,17). (32(34,36) sts)

MITTEN TOP

Work as for left mitten.

THUMB TOP

Work as for left mitten.

FLIP TOP

Work as for left mitten.

ROBIN TUMMY

Work as for left mitten.

FINISHING

Sew side seams of mitten and thumb seams. Sew side seam on flip top and sew cast off edge to top of mitten on one side. Sew button on to mitten under loop. Sew tummy on to flip top and embroider beak in a V-shape with yellow yarn. Sew buttons on to circles of white felt and attach for the eyes above the beak.

Owl Sweater,
Toy and Scarf

This sweater is worked from the top down, with stocking roll hem, owl pocket, scarf and matching toy. The sweater yoke is worked flat on a circular needle to accommodate the large number of stitches. The scarf can be made wider by casting on an additional even number of stitches.

Size: Toy: 8 x 9 cm (3 x 3½ in). Scarf: 11 x 70 cm (4½ x 27½ in). Sweater: 3–12 months (chest 46–48 cm/18–19 in); 12–18 months (chest 52–54 cm/20½–21¼ in). Sample shown is 12–18 months.

Yarn: Sweater: King Cole Fashion Aran (70% acrylic, 30% wool; 100 g/3½ oz; 200 m/218 yd) MC leaf green (shade 387) 200 g (7 oz).
Scarf: King Cole Fashion Aran (70% acrylic, 30% wool; 100 g/3½ oz; 200 m/ 218 yd) MC leaf green (shade 387) 150 g (5 oz).
Owl: Sirdar Hayfield Bonus DK (100% acrylic; 100 g/3½ oz; 280 m/306 yd) CC1 fox orange (shade 779) 50 g (2 oz); CC2 white (shade 961) 50 g (2 oz); CC3 bright lemon yellow (shade 819) 50 g (2 oz); CC4 light grey mix (shade 814) 50 g (2 oz).

Other materials: 3 buttons for the sweater (13 mm/¾ in diameter); 2 buttons (6 mm/¼ in diameter) and circles of white felt for the eyes; 100 g (3½ oz) toy filling for the toy

Needles: Sweater: 5 mm (US 8) 40 cm (16 in) circular needle and dpns. Owl: 3.5 mm (US 4) straight needles. Scarf: 5.5 mm (US 9) straight needles

Notions: Stitch holders

Tension: Sweater: 10 cm (4 in) square = 18 sts x 25 rows in stocking stitch on 5 mm (US 8) needles with MC

Construction: Worked flat and in the round

Skills needed: Brioche rib for scarf, intarsia colourwork for owl pocket and toy

Knitting Pattern

SWEATER

NOTE ON WORKING BUTTONHOLES
Work buttonholes at the start of Row 4 and then every 3 cm (1¼ in) on the button placket as follows: on the RS row, for first 5 sts of placket, K2, yo, K2tog, K1, then continue in pattern from *.

YOKE
With MC and 5 mm (US 8) circular needle cast on 54(54) sts.
Rows 1–5: K5, *P1, K1* to last 5 sts, K5.
On Row 5, PM after foll sts; 13 (front), next 6 (sleeve), next 16 (back), next 6 (sleeve), leaving 13 (front).
Row 6: [RS] K5, *K to 2 sts before marker, kfb, K1, sm, kfb, rep from * to last 5 sts, K5. (62 sts).
Row 7: [WS] K5, P to last 5 sts, K5.
Rep Rows 6 and 7 until you have 150(166) sts: 25(27) sts (front), 30(34) sts (sleeve), 40(44) sts (back), 30(34) sts (sleeve), 25(27) sts (front).
On the next RS row, slip the last 5 sts of placket on to a 5 mm (US 8) straight needle or dpn, hold this needle behind the buttonhole placket so they overlap, slip the 1st st off the circular needle on to the straight needle, and K2tog, rep with the rem 4 sts of the placket to join. Then *K to 2 sts before marker, kfb, K1, remove marker, put 30(34) sts for sleeve on stitch holder without working, cast on 3 sts at underarm, remove next marker, kfb; rep from * once, K to end of row and PM before placket sts to mark beg of next rnd. Then work body of sweater in the round and K all rnds until piece is 31(33) cm (12¼(13) in) long. Cast off.

SLEEVES

Transfer 30(34) sts from holder and K. Pick up 5 sts at underarm, switch to dpns and join in round. K all rnds until sleeve measures 19(21) cm (7½(8¼) in) long at the underarm. Cast off.

FINISHING

Sew buttons on to placket under the buttonholes.

OWL POCKET

With CC1 and 3.5 mm (US 4) straight needles, cast on 15 sts.
Row 1: [WS] P.
Row 2: [RS] K1, M1, K to last st, M1, K1. (17 sts)
Rep Rows 1 and 2 until you have 23 sts.
Starting and ending with a P row work St st for 9 rows, then work eye pattern in intarsia colourwork.

EYES

Row 1: [RS] CC1 K11, CC3 K1, CC1 K11.
Row 2: CC1 P10, CC3 P3, CC1 P10.
Row 3: CC1 ssk, K5, CC2 K3, CC3 K3, CC2 K3, CC1 K5, K2tog. (21 sts)
Row 4: CC1 P5, CC2 P5, CC3 P1, CC2 P5, CC1 P5.
Row 5: CC1 K4, CC2 K13, CC1 K4.
Row 6: CC1 P4, CC2 P13, CC1 P4.
Row 7: CC1 ssk, K2, CC2 K13, CC1 K2, K2tog. (19 sts)
Row 8: CC1 P4, CC2 P5, CC1 P1, CC2 P5, CC1 P4.
Row 9: CC1 K5, CC2 K3, CC1 K3, CC2 K3, CC1 K5.

TOP OF HEAD

Work all foll rows in CC1.
Rows 10 and 12: P.
Row 11: Ssk, K to last 2 sts, K2tog. (17 sts)
Row 13: K1, M1, K to last st, M1, K1. (19 sts)
Row 14: P.
Cast off. With CC4 embroider feathers in V-shapes. Sew on buttons for eyes. Sew pocket on front of sweater and embroider feet at bottom with CC3.

SCARF

With MC and 5.5 mm (US 9) straight needles cast on 20 sts.
Row 1: K1, *yo, sl1 pwise wyib, K1, rep from * to last st, K1. (29 sts)
Row 2: K1 *yo, sl1 pwise wyib, K2tog, rep from * to last st, K1. (29 sts)
Rep Row 2 to desired scarf length.
Foll row: K1, *P1, K2tog* to last st, K1.
Cast off.

OWL TOY

Make 2 pocket pieces with one piece worked in CC1 only for the back. Sew together around the edges and stuff with toy filling.

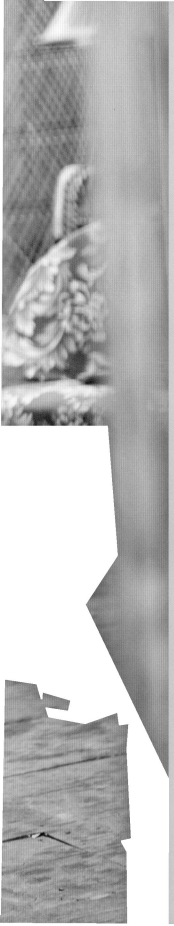

Chapter 7

Knitting Tutorials

The step-by-step illustrations and instructions in the following tutorials will guide you through the basic principles of knitting, from casting on and off to colour knitting techniques and shaping your work.

Casting on

At the start of knitting a project, you need to cast on the required number of stitches on to your knitting needles. Before casting on you will need to make a slipknot to anchor your yarn on to the needle and to create your first stitch.

MAKING A SLIPKNOT

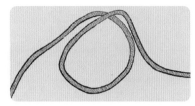

STEP 1 Holding the yarn tail in your left hand and the ball-end of the yarn in your right hand, make a small loop in the yarn.

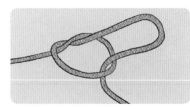

STEP 2 Take the end in your right hand underneath the loop and pull this through the first loop to make a slipknot.

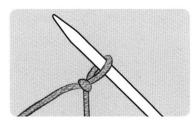

STEP 3 Place the loop of the slipknot on to the knitting needle and pull the yarn to finish the knot and make your first stitch.

CABLE CAST ON

The cable cast on creates a firm edge to your knitting.

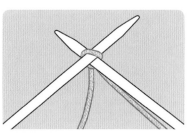

STEP 1 Make a slipknot. Hold the needle with the slipknot in your left hand and the ball-end of the yarn and the other knitting needle in your right hand. Insert the tip of the right needle into the slipknot on your left needle.

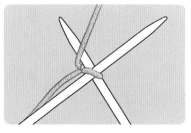

STEP 2 Wrap the yarn under and around the right-hand needle.

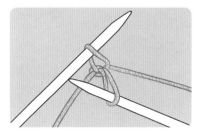

STEP 3 Bring the tip of the right-hand needle and the yarn wrapped around it through the stitch on the left-hand needle, bringing it towards you.

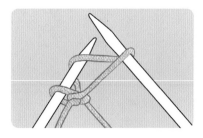

STEP 4 Slip this loop over the tip of the left-hand needle and pull the working yarn to create a new cast-on stitch.

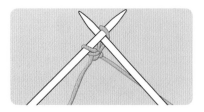

Make all the following stitches by inserting the right-hand needle between the last 2 stitches on the left-hand needle and follow Steps 2–4.

CONTINENTAL CAST ON

The continental cast on is also known as the long tail or double cast on and gives a stretchier edge to your knitting than the cable cast on. Before casting on, leave a tail four to five times the length of your cast-on edge, as both the yarn tail and yarn ball are used to cast on the stitches.

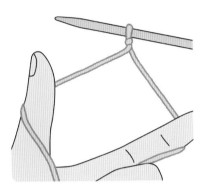

STEP 1 Make a slipknot on your right-hand needle and hold in your right hand.

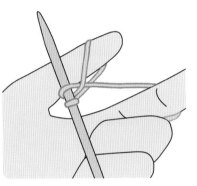

STEP 3 Bring the tip of the needle down and under the loop on your thumb from the bottom.

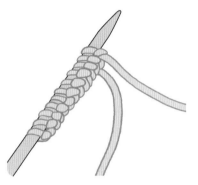

STEP 5 Drop the loop off your thumb to complete the stitch.

Repeat Steps 2–5 until the required number of stitches are cast on.

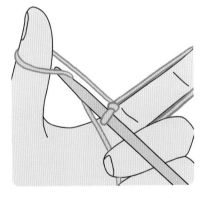

STEP 2 Hold the yarn in your left hand, with the yarn tail wrapped over and around your thumb, and the yarn ball wrapped over and around your index finger.

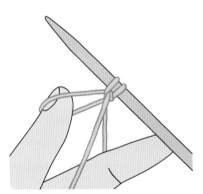

STEP 4 Bring the tip of the needle down through the loop on your index finger and then back up under the loop on your thumb.

 These instructions are for right-handed knitters. If you are a left-handed knitter, instead of casting on to the left-hand needle, cast on to the right-hand needle. Work with the left-hand needle while the right-hand one holds the stitches.

Knit and purl stitches

Knitted fabrics are made by knitting and purling stitches. Combinations of these stitches create different textures and patterns in your knitting.

KNIT

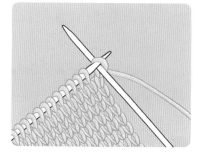

STEP 1 Place the needle holding the stitches in your left hand and the other in your right, with the working yarn at the back. Insert the tip of the right-hand needle into the first stitch near the tip of the left-hand needle, from front to back. Wrap yarn around the right-hand needle.

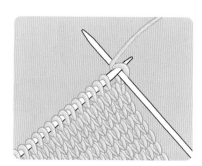

STEP 2 Insert the tip of the right-hand needle into the first stitch near the tip of the left-hand needle, inserting it from front to back. Wrap the working yarn around the right-hand needle.

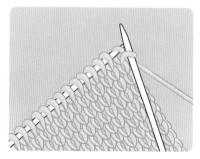

STEP 3 Pull this new loop on your right-hand needle through the stitch on your left-hand needle. Slide the first stitch on your left-hand needle so that it drops off the needle.

PURL

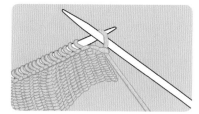

STEP 1 Place the needle holding the stitches in your left hand and the other needle in your right, with the working yarn at the front of the work Insert the tip of the right-hand needle into the first stitch near the tip of the left-hand needle, inserting it through the front from right to left.

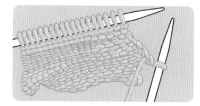

STEP 2 Wrap the working yarn over and around the right-hand needle.

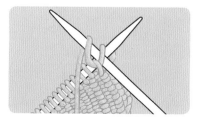

STEP 3 Pull this loop through the stitch on your left-hand needle. Slide the first stitch on this needle so it drops off.

Basic stitch patterns

Most stitch patterns are created by working a combination of knit and purl stitches.

RIBBED STITCH PATTERNS

Ribbed stitches make a stretchy fabric and are often used to work cuffs and hems.

To work a K1, P1 rib, knit the first stitch and purl the next, then repeat this sequence across the row. After each knit stitch, bring the yarn to the front of the work between the tips of the needles, ready to purl the next stitch. Similarly, after the purl stitch, take the yarn to the back of the work between the tips of the needles, ready to knit the next stitch. On the next row of ribbing, knit the knit stitches and purl the purl stitches.

A K2, P2 rib pattern follows the same principle, except you will knit 2 stitches, then purl 2 stitches, and repeat the sequence.

STOCKING STITCH

Abbreviated as St st, this is worked by alternating rows of purl and knit stitches in flat knitting. When knitting in the round, you will knit every round to work stocking.

Stocking fabric has a smooth right side (the knit side) and a bumpy wrong side (the purl side).

GARTER STITCH

Garter stitch is made by knitting every row when working flat, or when working in the round by working alternate knit and purl rounds. This makes a textured reversible fabric.

Purl   Knit

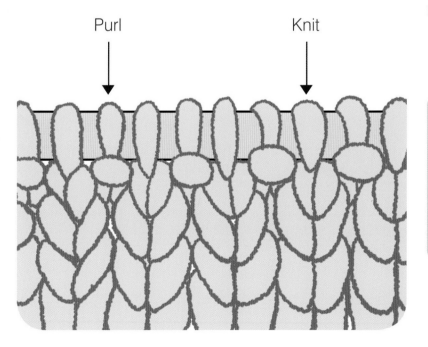

> *Tip* The purl stitches have a horizontal bar (a little bump) under the stitch on the needle. You will purl these stitches. The knit stitches don't have the bar underneath, so you knit these stitches.

Casting off

Casting off finishes the knitting and can be done in different ways.

CABLE CAST OFF

This is the most common cast off method.

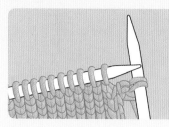

STEP 1 Knit the first two stitches.

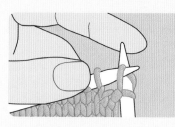

STEP 2 Insert the tip of the left-hand needle into the first stitch you knitted on the right-hand needle, lift it over the second stitch you knitted on the right-hand needle and drop it off.

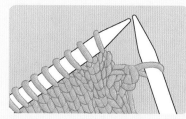

STEP 3 There is one stitch left. Knit the next stitch on left-hand needle.

Repeat Steps 2 and 3 until your stitches have been cast off.

STRETCHY CAST OFF

These cast offs give a stretchy edge to the knitting and are ideal for cuffs on mittens and socks. You can choose your preferred method.

The decrease or lacy cast off

Back of the loops version

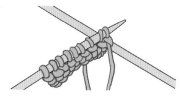

STEP 1 Knit together the first two stitches on the left-hand needle through the back of the loops.

STEP 2 Slip the new stitch on the right-hand needle back to the left-hand needle.

Repeat Steps 1 and 2 until all stitches are cast off.

Front of the loops version

STEP 1 Knit together the first two stitches on the left-hand needle through the front of the loops.

STEP 2 Slip the new stitch on the right-hand needle back to the left-hand needle. Repeat Steps 1 and 2 until all stitches are cast off.

The elastic cast off

STEP 1 Work the first stitch.

STEP 2 Where the next stitch to be worked is a knit stitch, knit the stitch on to the right-hand needle. Where the next stitch to be worked is a purl stitch, purl the next stitch.

STEP 3 For knit sts, insert the left-hand needle into the front of the two stitches on the right-hand needle and knit the two sts together through the back of the loops. For purl sts, insert the left-hand needle into the back of the two stitches on the right-hand needle and purl the two sts together.

Repeat Steps 2 and 3 until all sts are cast off.

GATHERED OR PULL-THROUGH CAST OFF

Gathering stitches to cast them off is often used to close the tops of hats.

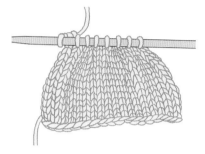

STEP 1 At the cast off edge, break the yarn leaving a long tail. Your tail should be as long as the knitting stitches, plus at least 30 cm (12 in). Thread the tail on to a darning or tapestry needle.

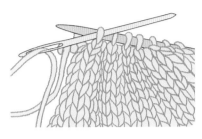

STEP 4 Repeat Steps 2 and 3 with all the stitches on your cast off edge, allowing them to fall off the needle one by one.

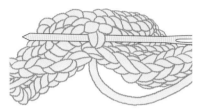

STEP 7 On the wrong side of the knitting, secure the thread. You can do this by sewing over a couple of stitches a few times on the wrong side. I like to use the rest of the tail to start sewing the side seams together (if that is what the pattern requires), as this helps secure the end.

STEP 2 Take the darning needle through the first live stitch on the knitting needle.

STEP 5 When you have finished, all your live stitches will be threaded on to the yarn tail.

The finished cast off.

STEP 3 Pull the darning needle all the way through the stitch and let the stitch fall off the knitting needle. The stitch is now threaded on your yarn tail, so don't worry, your knitting won't unravel!

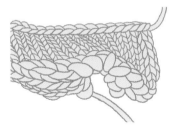

STEP 6 Pull the yarn tail and gather the stitches together so they bunch up to close the end of the knitting. Pull tight, but don't pull too much or you may break the yarn.

Shaping knitting

You can shape your knitting by increasing or decreasing the number of stitches on a row. Check the abbreviations in the pattern to use the correct technique for your project.

KFB INCREASE
Knit into the front and back of a stitch to increase by one stitch knitwise.

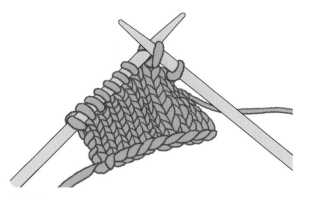

STEP 1 Work to the point of the increase. Knit the next stitch on the left-hand needle, but do not slip the original stitch off the left-hand needle.

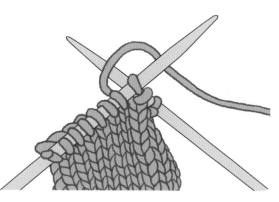

STEP 3 Pass the yarn under and around the tip of the right-hand needle (as you would when knitting a stitch).

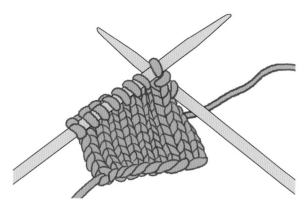

STEP 2 Insert the tip of the right-hand needle into the back of the same stitch on the left-hand needle.

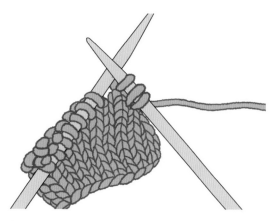

STEP 4 Bring the right needle and the yarn wrapped around it through the stitch on the left-hand needle. Now slip the original stitch off the left-hand needle and the increase is complete.

DOUBLE INCREASE KFBF

Follow the kfb instructions, but do not let the sts fall off the needle, then knit into the front of the same stitch again. You have now made two additional stitches (three stitches have been made out of one).

M1 INCREASE

Make one stitch between 2 stitches.

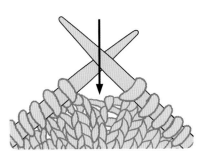

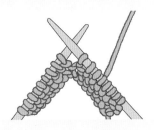

STEP 4 Remove the right-hand needle to place the strand on the left-hand needle.

STEP 1 Work to the position of the increase. Pull the needles apart and you will see a little horizontal bar (shown by the arrow in the picture above). You will use this bar to make your new stitch.

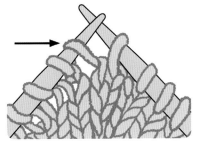

STEP 5 Knit into the back of the loop on the left-hand needle and allow the stitch to fall off the left-hand needle.

STEP 2 With the right-hand needle, lift the horizontal strand from the front.

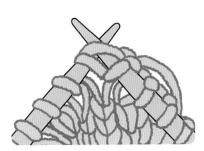

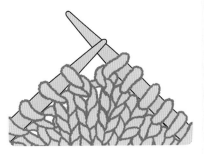

This increase slopes to the left on stocking stitch. To make a mirrored increase sloping right, pick up the strand from the back at Step 2, and knit into the front at Step 5.

STEP 3 Slip the tip of the left-hand needle under the right-hand needle and place the strand on the left-hand needle.

YO INCREASE

A yarnover increases by one stitch. Combining a yo with a K2tog creates a small buttonhole.

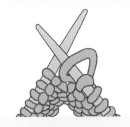

STEP 1 Work to the position of the yarnover.

STEP 2 Bring the yarn forwards between the tips of the needles.

STEP 3 Take the yarn backwards over the right-hand needle. After pulling the yarn you will have another 'stitch' on the right-hand needle. Work the next stitch as instructed in pattern.

Decreases

SSK DECREASE

Slip the next stitch on the left-hand needle knitwise, then slip the next stitch on the left-hand needle purlwise. Take the left-hand needle and knit through the front of the two slipped stitches on the right-hand needle.

An alternative to ssk is to decrease with skpo (slip, knit, pass over). To work a skpo, slip the next stitch on the left-hand needle knitwise, knit the next stitch on the left-hand needle, and then pass the slipped stitch on the right-hand needle over the knitted stitch on the right-hand needle.

SLIPPING STITCHES

Slipping a stitch moves it from the left-hand needle to the right-hand needle without knitting or purling the stitch.

To slip a stitch knitwise, from front to back, insert the tip of the right-hand needle into the stitch on the left-hand needle and slip it on to the right-hand needle. To slip a stitch purlwise, use the same method but insert the right-hand needle into the stitch from the back to the front.

K2TOG DECREASE

Knit two stitches together to make a single decrease.

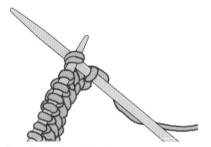

STEP 1 Work to the point of the decrease. Insert the right-hand needle through the next two stitches on the left-hand needle. Insert the needle from front to back as if you were knitting a normal stitch.

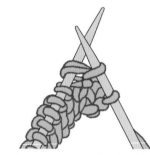

STEP 3 Pull the new loop on the right-hand needle through the two stitches on the left-hand needle.

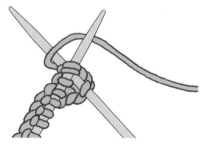

STEP 2 Pass the yarn under and around the tip of the right-hand needle (as you would when knitting a stitch).

STEP 4 Slip the two stitches off the left-hand needle and the decrease is completed.

Seaming

Take your time when sewing your knitting together and use a blunt tapestry or darning needle. Where possible, use the same yarn that you used to knit the pieces to stitch the seams.

MATTRESS STITCH

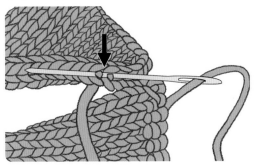

STEP 1 To join two edges of stocking stitch, lay the seams side by side, with the right side facing you. Thread a tapestry needle with yarn (at least 45 cm/18 in). To sew the seam, take the needle from the front under the 2 'bars' (the horizontal strands of the rows above).

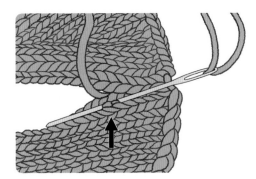

STEP 2 Take the needle across to the other side and from the front under the two bars on that side. Continue zigzagging between the two sides. As you sew, gently pull the stitches up to close the seam. Don't pull too tightly or the seam will pucker.

JOINING CAST ON AND CAST OFF EDGES

To join two cast off/cast on edges, lay the two pieces together right side facing outward. Bring the needle under the V-shape of the stitch on one side. Take the needle across to the other side and take under the V-shape of the stitch. Continue zigzagging across the work, pulling the seam closed as you sew.

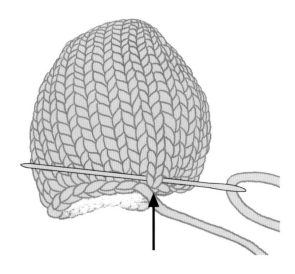

Short row shaping

Short rows make curves and are used for projects such as the snake toy on page 45. They are made by partially knitting a row, then turning the work and working back, then turning again. This adds partial rows to the knitting. Turning the knitting can leave small holes in your work at the point of the turn, so some patterns specify that you should wrap the next stitch at each turn point.

HOW TO WRAP AND TURN ON A KNIT ROW

STEP 1 Work to the point of the turn and then wrap the next stitch. To do this, slip purlwise from the left-hand needle to the right-hand needle.

STEP 3 Bring the working yarn between the tips of the two needles so it is at the front of the work.

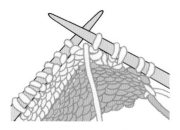

STEP 5 Take the working yarn from the front to the back of the work between the tips of the two needles; this 'wraps' the stitch.

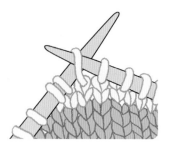

STEP 2 Check that working yarn is at the back of the work and the stitch has now slipped from the left- to the right-hand needle.

STEP 4 Pass the slipped stitch from the right-hand needle back on to the left-hand needle.

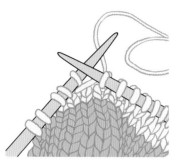

STEP 6 Now turn the work so the purl side is facing you.

HOW TO WRAP AND TURN ON A PURL ROW

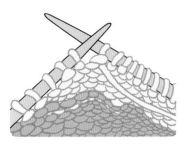

STEP 1 Work to the point of the turn and then wrap the next stitch.

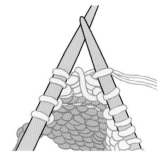

STEP 2 Slip the next stitch purlwise from the left-hand needle to the right-hand needle with the working yarn at the front of the work.

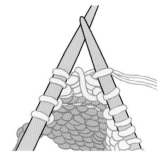

STEP 3 Take the working yarn to the back of the work between the tips of the two needles.

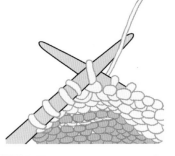

STEP 4 Pass the slipped stitch from the right-hand needle back on to the left-hand needle.

STEP 5 Take the working yarn from the back to the front of the work between the tips of the two needles; this 'wraps' the stitch.

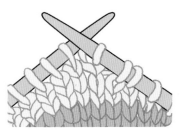

STEP 6 Now turn the work so the knit side is facing you.

PICKING UP WRAPS ON A KNIT ROW

The wrap lies horizontally across the stitch. Pick up this wrap with the right-hand needle from front to back.

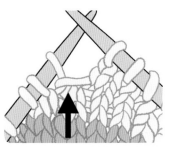

STEP 1 The wrapped stitch is on the front row.

STEP 2 Pick up the wrap from front to back.

STEP 3 Insert the right-hand needle into the stitch that is wrapped on the left-hand needle and knit the wrap and the stitch together.

PICKING UP WRAPS ON A PURL ROW

It is easier to spot the wrapped stitch from the right side (knit side) of the work, as you can see the horizontal wrap around the stitch more clearly. From the wrong side (purl side) pick up the wrap with the right-hand needle from back to front.

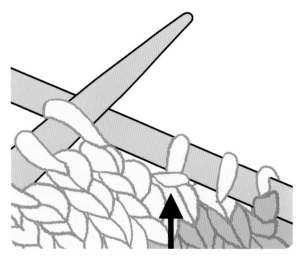

STEP 1 The wrapped stitch can be viewed from the right side (knit side).

STEP 3 Place the wrap on the left-hand needle.

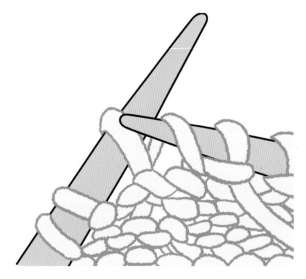

STEP 2 Pick up the wrap from back to front.

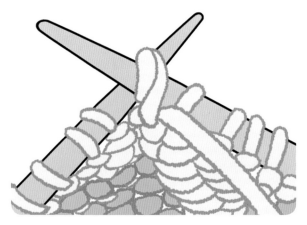

STEP 4 Purl together the stitch that is wrapped and the wrap that was just placed on the needle (just like purling two stitches together).

I-cord

An I-cord is a knitted tube that is worked on two double pointed needles (dpns).

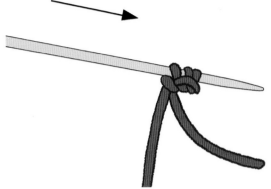

STEP 1 Cast on the required no. of stitches on one dpn. With the cast on stitches on the left-hand needle, knit one row using the other dpn as your right-hand needle (just like regular knitting). The working yarn is at the left-hand end of the needle (as shown in the picture above).

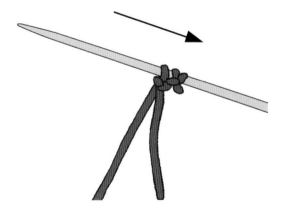

STEP 2 At this point in regular knitting you would turn the work. To make an I-cord, you do not turn.

Slide the stitches from the left-hand end of the needle to the right-hand end of the needle before knitting the next row.

STEP 3 Hold the needle with the stitches on it in your left hand. The working yarn is at the left-hand end of the needle (not the right-hand end as it would normally be with regular knitting).

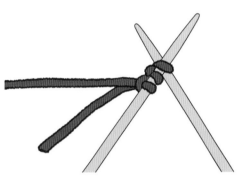

STEP 4 Knit the first stitch on the left-hand needle, pulling the working yarn up firmly behind the stitches (at the back of the work). This pull will bring the edges of the knitting together to form a tube.

Ensure your first stitch is tight; otherwise the I-cord may look baggy. Knit the rem stitches as normal. The working yarn is at the left-hand end of the needle.

Repeat Steps 2, 3 and 4 for a few rows, sliding the knitted stitches from one end of the needle to the other before knitting each row. Then pull down gently on the cast-on edge at the bottom of the cord as this helps to form a neat tube.

Once your I-cord is the desired length, cut the yarn, thread it through the stitches on the needle and pull tightly to cast off.

Making toy eyes

I use buttons for the eyes of my toys, but do make sure these are firmly sewn on to your knitting so that they cannot be pulled off and swallowed. You can use safety toy eyes if you prefer – these are fastened on the back of the knitting with a washer but are sometimes not recommended for children under 36 months. Check with the manufacturer or retailer if you are in any doubt before using. For babies and younger children, embroidering the eyes with wool is the safest option.

HOW TO MAKE TOY EYES

STEP 1 Use a length of yarn approximately 45 cm (18 in) long (I have used a shorter length here so it is easier to see in close up). Make a loop in the centre of the length of yarn, with the right-hand end lying over the top (the right-hand end is the working end).

STEP 2 Take the working end over and up through the centre of the loop to make a loose knot.

STEP 3 Continue to wind the working end through the loose knot.

STEP 4 The more times you wind, the larger the final knot will be. I usually wind a total of five times.

STEP 5 Hold on to each end of the yarn and pull the knot tight. The loops bunch together as you pull.

STEP 6 You should finish with a knot in the centre of the length of the wool.

To attach the eyes, thread a tapestry needle on to one of the ends and sew in position on the toy's face with the knot on top (the right-side of the knitting) and the loose end on the inside (wrong-side). Repeat with the other end of the yarn. Tie the two ends together inside the toy's head and hide the loose ends inside the stuffing.

Colourwork

KNITTING STRIPES

When knitting stripes, you will need to join a new ball of yarn at the edge of the knitting.

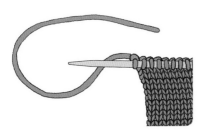

STEP 1 At the end of the row, cut the yarn leaving a tail about 20 cm (8 in) long.

STEP 2 At the beginning of the next row, slip the tip of the right-hand needle into the first stitch on the left-hand needle in the usual way. Loop the new yarn around the tip of the right-hand needle.

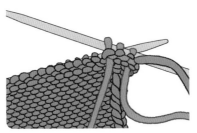

STEP 3 Work the first three or four stitches on the row using the new yarn, keeping hold of the tails at the end of the row as you knit so that your stitches do not unravel. After knitting the few stitches, tie the tail ends in a knot to secure at the end of the row. Continue knitting the row as normal with the new colour.

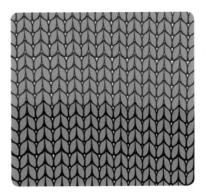

STEP 4 When you have finished knitting, you would usually sew or weave in the ends. However, if you are making toys the ends are usually hidden inside the toy, so you can skip this step – just make sure your ends are securely knotted and hide the tails inside the toy when stuffing.

FAIR ISLE KNITTING

Fair Isle or stranded knitting is a technique for working two or more colours in the same row. To work Fair Isle you carry the colour of yarn you are not knitting across the back of the work as you go, picking it up when you need it. This leaves a strand of yarn at the back of the work.

Following the pattern, work the stitches in the main colour (MC), then knit the stitches with your contrasting colour (CC). Add a new colour following the instructions for adding a new colour at the edge of your knitting, and leave a tail for weaving in on the wrong side.

When changing colours, pick up the new colour from underneath the yarn you just finished knitting to twist the yarns together and prevent holes in the fabric. Don't pull too tightly as this can bunch up and pucker the knitting.

INTARSIA KNITTING

With intarsia knitting, instead of stranding the unused colour at the back of the work as with Fair Isle, you will stop and knit with the new colour and leave the unused colour hanging at the back of the work to pick up on the next row. Bobbins are useful here.

Following the pattern, work the stitches in the main colour (MC), then drop this at the back of the work and change to the new colour (CC), bringing it up underneath the old one to twist the strands and prevent holes forming.

Tension

Tension is the number of stitches and rows measured in centimetres or inches.

TO CHECK TENSION
If the tension quoted is, for example, 10 cm (4 in) square = 14 sts x 20 rows on 6 mm (US 10) needles in stocking stitch:
Cast on the number of stitches given plus 4 (i.e. 18 stitches) and work in stocking stitch for 4 rows more than the number stated (i.e. 24 rows). Break the yarn leaving a 30 cm (12 in) tail and thread this end through the stitches, then remove them from the knitting needle. Don't cast off as this can distort the stitches.

TO COUNT THE STITCHES
Place a pin vertically into the knitting 2 stitches from one side edge. Measure 10 cm (4 in) from this pin and insert a second pin, then count the stitches. A stitch makes a V-shape and each V counts as one stitch.

TO COUNT THE ROWS
Place a ruler vertically on the square and insert a pin at the bottom of one stitch and another pin 10 cm (4 in) away. Count the V shapes between the two pins.

If you have too few stitches/rows, change to smaller needles. If you have too many stitches/rows, change to larger needles and make another tension swatch.

Picking up stitches

When you are picking up stitches on the side of your knitting, bear in mind that you will generally not pick up a stitch for every row because knitting stitches are not square.

So, if the knitted piece is worked in stocking stitch you would generally pick up 3 stitches for every 4 rows on the side edge, whereas if it was a garter stitch piece you would generally pick up 1 stitch for every 2 rows on the side edge, although this will depend on the tension of the knitting.

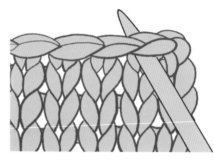

STEP 1 With the right side facing you, insert the knitting needle into the corner stitch of the first row, one stitch in from the side edge. Wrap the yarn around the needle knitwise.

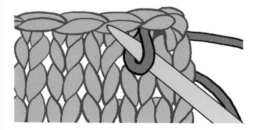

STEP 2 Draw the yarn through to pick up one stitch. Continue to pick up stitches along the edge, skipping rows occasionally to keep the knitting even.

Knitting in the round

Knitting in the round creates a tubular shape and is used for knitting seamless hats, socks and so on. There are several techniques for knitting in the round; the most common uses double pointed needles (dpns), but you can also use circular needles to knit in the round for larger pieces, and knit smaller pieces using the magic loop method. A stitch marker is really handy to mark the end of each round, so you don't lose your place in the pattern.

When you are knitting in the round, you are always working on the right side of the fabric. To work stocking stitch you will knit every round, but to work garter stitch you will knit and purl alternate rounds.

Knitting in the round can be tricky for new knitters, so please don't give up if you can't do it right away. I find knitting in the round on dpns cumbersome and I always revert to the magic loop method.

USING DPNS

Cast on the number of stitches on to one needle and then slip about one-third of the stitches purlwise on to a second dpn, and repeat with a third dpn, so the stitches are almost equally divided across the three needles.

With the cast-on edge pointing down on all needles, and making sure the stitches are not twisted, push the stitches on the left-hand needle down to the tip closest to you and insert the fourth dpn into the first stitch on the left-hand needle to join in the round. Continue to knit across each of the needles.

THE MAGIC LOOP METHOD

This is my preferred method of knitting in the round, with the added advantage that you only need to buy one circular needle.

You will need a long circular needle (60–80 cm/24–30 in is ideal) and cast on the number of stitches needed. Slide the stitches on to the bendy cable part of the circular needle, then halfway down the stitches bend the cable and slide the stitches back on to the needles. You should have roughly an even number of stitches on each needle with a loop of cable at the halfway point. With your working yarn hanging at the back needle, use that needle tip to work the stitches at the front, making sure the stitches are not twisted. Knit all the stitches on the front needle and continue around the back needle to knit one round.

USING CIRCULAR NEEDLES

To knit larger pieces in the round using a circular needle, cast on the required number of stitches and slide to the tip of the left-hand needle. Making sure your stitches are not twisted, hold the right-hand needle and join the round by knitting each stitch.

Reference charts

Clothing

Size	3 months	6 months	12 months	18 months	24 months
Chest	40.5 cm 16 in	43 cm 17 in	45.5 cm 18 in	48 cm 19 in	50.5 cm 20 in
Neck to cuff centre back	26.5 cm 10.5 in	29 cm 11.5 in	31.5 cm 12.5 in	35.5 cm 14 in	45.5 cm 18 in
Back waist length	15.5 cm 6 in	17.5 cm 7 in	19 cm 7.5 in	20.5 cm 8 in	21.5 cm 8.5 in
Cross back shoulder to shoulder	18.5 cm 7.25 in	19.5 cm 7.5 in	21 cm 8.25 in	21.5 cm 8.5 in	22 cm 8.75 in
Sleeve length to underarm	15.5 cm 6 in	16.5 cm 6.5 in	19 cm 7.5 in	20.5 cm 8 in	21.5 cm 8.5 in
Upper arm	14 cm 5.5 in	15.5 cm 6 in	16.5 cm 6.5 in	17.5 cm 7 in	19 cm 7.5 in
Armhole depth	8.5 cm 3.25 in	9 cm 3.5 in	9.5 cm 3.75 in	10 cm 4 in	10.5 cm 4.25 in
Waist	45.5 cm 18 in	48 cm 19 in	50.5 cm 20 in	52 cm 20.5 in	53.5 cm 21 in
Hips	48 cm 19 in	50.5 cm 20 in	50.5 cm 20 in	53.5 cm 21 in	56 cm 22 in
Leg length waist to ankle	36 cm 14 in	42 cm 16.5 in	46 cm 18 in	49 cm 19.25 in	52 cm 20.5 in

Hats

Age	Head circumference	Hat height
Newborn	33–36 cm/13–14 in	13–15 cm/5.5–6 in
3–6 months	36–43 cm/14–17 in	15–18 cm/6.5–7 in
6–12 months	41–48 cm/16–19 in	18 cm/7.5 in
12–36 months	46–48 cm/18–20 in	20 cm/8 in

Shoes

Age	Foot length
Newborn	9–10 cm/3.25–3.75 in
3–6 months	10–12 cm/4–4.5 in
6–12 months	12–13 cm/4.25–4.75 in
18–24 months	13–14 cm/4.5–5.5 in
24–48 months	14–15 cm/5.5–6 in

ABBREVIATIONS

General abbreviations

alt	alternate
approx	approximate(ly)
beg	beginning
CC	contrast colour
cm	centimetres
cont	continue
dec(s)	decrease(s)
DK	double knit yarn
dpn(s)	double pointed needle(s)
foll	follow(ing)
in(s)	inch(es)
inc(s)	increase(s)
LH	left-hand
m	metre
MC	main colour
mm	milimetres
no.	number
PM	place marker
rem	remaining
rep	repeat
RH	right-hand
rnd(s)	round(s)
RS	right side
sm	slip marker
st(s)	stitch(es)
St st	stocking stitch
WS	wrong side
yd	yard

Knitting stitches abbreviations

byf	bring yarn to the front
C4B	cable four back
C4F	cable four front
K	knit
K2tog tbl decrease	knit two stitches together through the back of the loops
K2tog	knit two stitches together decrease
K3tog tbl decrease	knit three stitches together through the back of the loops
K3tog	knit three stitches together decrease
kfb	knit front and back increase
kfbf	knit into the front and back and front again of the next st for a double increase
kwise	knitwise
M1	make one increase
P	purl
P2tog	purl two stitches together decrease
psso	pass slipped stitch over
pwise	purlwise
sl1	slip one stitch
ssk	slip slip knit decrease
turn	turn the work part way through the row
tyb	take yarn to the back
w&t	wrap and turn
wyib	with the yarn in the back of the work
wyif	with the yarn in the front of the work
yo	yarnover

KNITTING NEEDLE CONVERSION CHART

US size	metric
3	3.25 mm
4	3.5 mm
5	3.75 mm
6	4 mm
7	4.5 mm
8	5 mm
9	5.5 mm
10	6 mm
10.5	6.5 mm
15	10 mm

YARN TYPES CHART

Yarn is available in a wide range of weights and fibres. For baby projects, I recommend that machine washable yarns are used – the yarn band should give you the washing instructions. Avoid fluffy yarns such as eyelash or mohair, as these have fibres that could be pulled off and swallowed by young children. The projects in this book use four types of yarn, and the table below gives more details.

yarn	also known as	ply
Double Knit (DK)	light worsted, sport	5–8 ply
Aran	worsted, fisherman, medium, afghan	8–10 ply
Chunky	bulky, craft, rug	12–16 ply
Super chunky	super bulky, roving	20 ply

YARN BAND DETAILS

To help you choose the yarn for your knits, here are the details of the yarns used for the projects in this book. They will help you to choose alternative yarns for all the items. Please note, for toys I tend to use a smaller needle size than recommended on the band to make a denser fabric so that the stuffing doesn't show through. All yarn was sourced at **deramores.com.**

King Cole Big Value Chunky

Yarn weight and blend:	**Chunky; 100% acrylic**
Yarn band suggested needle size:	6 mm (US 10)
Yarn band suggested tension:	10 cm (4 in) square = 14 sts x 20 rows in stocking stitch
Ball weight/length:	100 g (3½ oz) 152 m (166 yd)

King Cole Big Value DK

Yarn weight and blend:	**DK (double knit); 100% acrylic**
Yarn band suggested needle size:	4 mm (US 6)
Yarn band suggested tension:	10 cm (4 in) square = 22 sts x 28 rows in stocking stitch
Ball weight/length:	100 g (3½ oz) 290 m (317 yd)

King Cole Cottonsoft DK

Yarn weight and blend:	**DK (double knit); 100% cotton**
Yarn band suggested needle size:	4 mm (US 6)
Yarn band suggested tension:	10 cm (4 in) square = 22 sts x 28 rows in stocking stitch
Ball weight/length:	100 g (3½ oz) 210 m (229 yd)

King Cole Fashion Aran

Yarn weight and blend:	**Aran; 70% acrylic, 30% wool**
Yarn band suggested needle size:	5 mm (US 8)
Yarn band suggested tension:	10 cm (4 in) square = 18 sts x 25 rows in stocking stitch
Ball weight/length:	100 g (3½ oz) 200 m (218 yd)

Lion Brand Hometown USA—Multi

Yarn weight and blend:	**Super Chunky; 100% acrylic**
Yarn band suggested needle size:	9 mm (US 13)
Yarn band suggested tension:	10 cm (4 in) square = 9 sts x 12 rows in stocking stitch
Ball weight/length:	113 g (4 oz) 59 m (64 yd)

Patons Wool Blend Aran

Yarn weight and blend:	**Aran; Wool mix**
Yarn band suggested needle size:	4.5 mm (US 7)
Yarn band suggested tension:	10 cm (4 in) square = 19 sts x 25 rows in stocking stitch
Ball weight/length:	100 g (3½ oz) 185 m (202 yd)

Rowan British Sheep Breeds Chunky Undyed

Yarn weight and blend:
Yarn band suggested needle size:
Yarn band suggested tension:
Ball weight/yardage:

Chunky; 100% wool
7 mm (US 10½)
10 cm (4 in) square = 13 sts x 18 rows in stocking stitch
100 g (3½ oz) 110 m (120 yd)

Rowan Pure Wool DK

Yarn weight and blend:
Yarn band suggested needle size:
Yarn band suggested tension:
Ball weight/yardage:

DK (double knit); 100% wool
4 mm (US 6)
10 cm (4 in) square = 22 sts x 30 rows in stocking stitch
50 g (2 oz) 125 m (137 yd)

Sirdar Country Style DK

Yarn weight and blend:
Yarn band suggested needle size:
Yarn band suggested tension:
Ball weight/yardage:

DK (double knit); 40% nylon, 30% wool, 30% acrylic
4 mm (US 6)
10 cm (4 in) square = 22 sts x 28 rows in stocking stitch
50 g (2 oz) 155 m (170 yd)

Sirdar Hayfield Bonus DK

Yarn weight and blend:
Yarn band suggested needle size:
Yarn band suggested tension:
Ball weight/yardage:

DK (double knit); 100% acrylic
4 mm (US 6)
10 cm (4 in) square = 22 sts x 28 rows in stocking stitch
100 g (3½ oz) 280 m (306 yd)

Sirdar Snuggly Snowflake Chunky
Yarn weight and blend:
Yarn band suggested needle size:
Yarn band suggested tension:
Ball weight/yardage:

Chunky; 100% polyester
5.5 mm (US 9)
10 cm (4 in) square = 14 sts x 19 rows in stocking stitch
25 g (1 oz) 62 m (68 yd)

Stylecraft Special Aran
Yarn weight and blend:
Yarn band suggested needle size:
Yarn band suggested tension:
Ball weight/yardage:

Aran; 100% acrylic
5 mm (US 8)
10 cm (4 in) square = 18 sts x 24 rows in stocking stitch
100 g (3½ oz) 196 m (214 yd)

Stylecraft Special Chunky
Yarn weight and blend:
Yarn band suggested needle size:
Yarn band suggested tension:
Ball weight/yardage:

Chunky; 100% acrylic
6 mm (US 10)
10 cm (4 in) square = 14 sts x 20 rows in stocking stitch
100 g (3½ oz) 144 m (157 yd)

Index

A QUINTET BOOK

First published in the UK in 2015 by
Apple Press
74-77 White Lion Street
London N1 9PF
United Kingdom
www.apple-press.com

ISBN: 978-1-84543-602-5

QTT.AKFK

Conceived, designed and produced by:
Quintet Publishing
4th Floor, Sheridan House
114–116 Western Road
Hove BN3 1DD
United Kingdom

Project Editor: Caroline Elliker
Designer: Anna Gatt
Photographer: Jessica Morgan
Art Director: Michael Charles
Editorial Director: Emma Bastow
Publisher: Mark Searle

Manufactured in China by 1010 Printing International Ltd.

9 8 7 6 5 4 3 2 1

About the author

Amanda Berry lives in Berkshire, England with her husband and a menagerie of knitted animals!

She was taught the basics of knitting by her mother at a young age (one of her first successful projects was a sweater for her teddy bear), but it was over twenty years before she rediscovered her love of the craft.

With a renewed passion for knitting and design, she left a career in accountancy to enrol in a degree course at London College of Fashion and began designing knitting patterns as 'fluff and fuzz' in 2010. From small beginnings, 'fluff and fuzz' grew to a selection of over fifty toy knitting patterns that are available online from knitting and craft websites including Ravelry, Folksy and Etsy.

Amanda's popular toy and accessory patterns have since been featured in publications including *Let's Get Crafting* and *Let's Knit* magazines.

As a predominantly self-taught knitter, Amanda understands that to new knitters some techniques can be scary, and she shares tips, techniques and photo tutorials through her knitting blog (*fluffandfuzzknitting.wordpress.com*) to help newbie knitters along the way.

Because she is a big kid at heart, when she isn't knitting, Amanda loves watching cartoons and walking by the River Thames, feeding the ducks. She loves to knit because each project is an opportunity to learn a new skill, create something unique and adapt patterns quite easily to suit her taste. Her favourite thing to do while knitting is to drink lots of tea and watch old movies!

Acknowledgements

I would like to thank everyone for their help in making this book, especially the wonderful folks at Quintet who have been so amazing, and also Ella and the great team at *Let's Get Crafting* magazine who have been so supportive. But most of all, I have to say a huge 'thank you' to my Mum for teaching me how to knit, and an extra special big thanks to my long-suffering but wonderful husband who has put up with piles of knitting stacking up all over our house for several months… John, you are a star!

Models

Indie May Bridgeman
Yusuf Charles
Blake Emami
Jem Harris
Faith Hinds

Liam Kapur
Roman Lovell
Ruby de Burgh Leather
Lottie-Warick Johnson
Alfie Pattison